Alfred Heaton Cooper

Painter of Landscape

Misty Autumn Morning, Newby Bridge

Alfred Heaton Cooper

Painter of Landscape

by

Jane Renouf

Red Bank Press

Published 1997 by
Red Bank Press
The Heaton Cooper Studio
Grasmere
Ambleside
Cumbria LA22 9SX
England

ISBN 0 9529963 0 8

ACKNOWLEDGEMENTS

The author and publishers gratefully acknowledge reproduction permission from the following:
The Clausen family & Professor K McConkey for the *The Stone Pickers*
Peter Hawarth for *The Shepherd, Coniston*
The late Dr. Madge for *Bad News from the Cape*
John Marsh for *Windermere Station* photographs
Robert Maynard for *Coniston Fells at Dawn*
Robert Opie, Gloucester Packaging Museum for *Skippers Sardines* label illustration

and would like to thank the following for contributions, advice and assistance:
Joan Cottam, Terry Gifford, Paul Harris, David Hill, Rachel Moss, Molly Strickland

List Of Books Illustrated compiled with the help of *The A & C Black Colour Books: A Collectors Guide & Bibliography* by Colin Inman, published by Werner Shaw

Art Editors: Julian & John Heaton Cooper
Editing, design and typesetting by Lynne Wilkinson & Paul Renouf

Contents

List of colour plates vi
List of sketches viii
List of photographs ix

INTRODUCTION xi

CHAPTER ONE - *page 1*
A Boltonian at Home 1863-1884

CHAPTER TWO - *page 13*
London, a Student of Life and Art 1884-1889

CHAPTER THREE - *page 35*
Norway, a Love Affair 1889-1894

CHAPTER FOUR - *page 57*
Hard Times 1894-1906

CHAPTER FIVE - *page 81*
Painter and Provider 1906-1920

CHAPTER SIX - *page 113*
Travels 1920-1926

CHAPTER SEVEN - *page 131*
Cross Brow, Ambleside 1926-1929

EPILOGUE - *page 151*

Family Tree (abridged) - *page 11*
List of paintings in Public Galleries - *page 151*
List of paintings accepted for Royal Academy Exhibitions - *page 152*
List of books illustrated - *page 153*
Index to text references - *page 154*

List of colour plates

A H Illingworth at Wetherall, *1922* 139
Abisko, Lake Torneträsk, *1926* 126
Alfred's oil palette 93
Alfred's Studio by the Thames at Old Windsor, *1886* 23
Annet Street, Pimlico - evening study in black and white, *1884* 20
At Balholm, *1891* 42
Autumn Afternoon on the Rothay 102
Bad News from the Cape, *1887* 32
Balholm in Autumn 59
Beda, *1894* 53
Bield, Little Langdale 114
Bristol from Clifton Observatory 84
Cactus in Battersea Park *1885* 20
Café, at Porjus, *1926* 127
Children of the Mist, Braemar, *1922* 138
Church Hill, Hawkshead, *1902* 66
City Hall, Stockholm, *1926* 124
Coniston (with the new studio in red) *1905* 71
Coniston Fells at Dawn, *1904* 80
Coniston from How Head, *1898* 83
Coniston Hunt - Red Screes, *1920* 90
Cooperhus now 77
Cottage Interior, Glencoyne Farm, Ullswater 89
Deane Church, *1892* 52
Dungeon Ghyll, Great Langdale, *1905* 141
Dyer's wife, The 43
Eiger and Monch, dawn, *1921* 115
Ellide, portrait by Mrs Collingwood 73
Feeding the Hens, Lowfold, Ambleside, *1926* 143
Figures at Whitby Market, *1921* 121
Flag Day, Lord Street, Southport, *1896* 56
Flag Street, Hawkshead, *1902* 64
Flowing to the Lake, Coniston 74
Fredericksborg Castle, Copenhagen, *1926* 118
Gate at the Kasba, *1888* 30
Girl sweeping 39
Goddsund, Hardanger Fjord, *1891* 36
Great Gable and Sprinkling Tarn 134
Gribscoven, the King's Pavilion Lake, *1926* 128
Halliwell Glen *1883* 9
Harspränget Falls, Gripsholm, *1926* 125
Hawkshead Old Hall and Courthouse, *1902* 66
Haycutting, Grasmere 104
Haymaking near Chorley 12
Helga 38
Herring curing Houses, East Cliff, Whitby, *1921* 119
Hopfield, Kent, *1895* 95
Horning, Norfolk Broads, *1919* 88
Humming Birds 4
Hunter's Return on long ski 42
Irish Cottage Interior, Achill Island, *1915* 86
Joiner's Shop, Haws Bank, Coniston, *1900* 138
Jönköping, *1926* 123
Jostedal Glacier, Fjærland Fjord 48
Kitchen at the Ship Inn, Coniston, *1905* 75
Lady "C . . ." 61
Lakeland Waterfall 14

Lancashire cornfield 51
Langdale Pikes from Oak Howe Farm 97
Launchy Ghyll, Thirlmere 105
Levers Water, *1900* 72
Maid with eggs 133
Misty Autumn Morning, Newby Bridge *Frontispiece*
Moonlight, Windermere, *1906* 106
Morning sun, Holme Point, Lake Windermere 107
Night train to Blackpool, *1895* 16
Old Elvet Bridge, Durham 88
Old Souk, Tangiers, *1888* 28
Oslo, Karl Johan Street, *1926* 87
Our Studio Villa, Balholm, Norway, *1907* x
Page by Alfred in Mathilde Valentinsen's autograph book, *1891* 44
Piers Ghyll from Gable, *1923*, 109
Piers Ghyll from Gable, *1923*, (by William Heaton Cooper) 109
Pillar from Scarth Gap, *1910* 135
Pillar Rock of Ennerdale,*1905* 140
Porlock Church 84
Rock of Cashel, Co. Tipperary, *1915* 118
Romsdal Fjord from Noes 39
Rydal Valley (pastel sketch), *1913* 91
Rydal Water 69
Saeter near Odde. *1891* 36
Seatoller, foot of Honister Pass 130
Shaftesbury, Gold Hill, *1925* 89
Shepherd, Coniston, *1903* 92
Showers over Garburn Pass, *1927* 145
Skjæggedalfos, Hardanger Fjord, *1905* 34
Smithy Brow, Ambleside 91
Sogn, Fjærlands, *1906* 94
Staithes (after the boats come in), *1921* 120
Stone Pickers by George Clausen, *1887* 19
Student drawings *1885* 13
Sverre at six months 60
Tjugum village, *1891* 94
Ullswater, stormy day 91
Ullswater, the Silver Strand, *1904* 85
Vadstena Castle, Sweden, *1926* 123
Wedding of Johannes Ese, *1892* 46
Whitby Abbey, *1921* 119
Windermere, lakeside and boats 63
Wood Farm, Troutbeck 98
Wrynose Pass and Cockley Beck xiv
Zermatt, *1921* 112

List of sketches (Pencil and Pen)

A.H.Illingworth at Wetherall, *1922* 139

Alfred's digs at Cheyne walk, Chelsea, *1885* 21

Alfred's Studio by the Thames at Old Windsor *1886* 23

All among the barley, *1879* 6

Benson Village, near Oxford, *1887* 26

Camels in the Soko 30

Carriole 37

Charcoal Burners at Bouth *1908* 17

Charcoal burners preparing the pit 65

Cliveden Woods from the backwater where we camped, *1887* 25

Coal and Iron versus Corn - Wigan, *1892* 50

Evening meal, *1897* 67

Fanden, Alfred's dog 54

From an etching by Turner in Ruskin's "Works" Vol.V *1879* 6

"George", houseboat on the Thames, *1887* 25

Going to the Bath, *1887* 24

Goode's boat sheds, Cambridge, *1894* 52

Grassington Market Place, *1889* 31

Hawkshead (moonlight) 12 November *1898* 62

Herr Haffner sketching, *1891* 40

Hotel Central, Tangiers 28

Interior of charcoal burners' hut, Bouth *1908* 65

Lapplander, *1926* 126

Loading and carting timber, Holker Park, *1890* 64

Log House studio (bottom left) 132

Lord and Master 60

Mathilde and Ellide, by the fireside, *1897* 67

Matterhorn from near Zermatt, *1921* 116

Meditation, *1885* 21

Norske Bergtrol! 41

Norske Kringle 38

Old boathouse lock 36

Old Fell Gate, Esthwaite 110

Old Well at Dorchester *1887* 26

On board *"SS Malta" 1888* 27

On the Datchet Road, near Windsor *1886* 24

Panel on board SS Fjaler 41

Peace, after John Ruskin from "Modern Painter" 7

Piers Ghyll, *1923* 108

Porridge stirrer 37

Reapers 18

Scythe 38

Sheep in Battersea Park *1886* 22

Ship Inn kitchen 75

Sledge 37

Soko Gate, Tangier 29

Study of boats at Lymm, 1879 6

Theatre Royal, Drury Lane, before and after the fire, *1884* 19

"There is a Reaper whose name is Death", *1894* 54

Thornton Force, Ingleton 32

Towards Tjugum Church, *1892* 57

'Vikings!' 36

Wet Day in the Bells of Ouzeley *1886* 22

While baby is asleep, *1897* 68

William Cooper, *1895* 61

List of photographs

Alfred, *1915* 101
Alfred and family at home in Norway, *1906* 76
Alfred and Mathilde at the Log House, *1913* 100
Alfred as a young man, *1885* 13
Alfred at Coniston, *1906* xiii
Alfred at the Log House studio, *1927* 132
Alfred with Painting 148
Alfred's oil palette 93
Balholm Villa 32
Book "The Norwegian Fjords" 82
Books illustrated by Alfred for A & C Black 70
Cooperhus now 77
Coopers' house in Markland Hill Lane (now demolished) *1975* 2
Dressing up - William (right) and Frithjof (left) 76
Edith and husband, Jean B. Gautreau 84
Ellide marries Harold Carson Parker, pictured at the Log House studio, Ambleside, *1917* 99
Frithjof *1914* 99
Grasmere Studio under construction, *1938*
Grasmere Studio *1996*
Log House Studio, *1930's* 132
Mathilde and Ellide, *1897* 67
'Norwegian' Studio, Coniston, *1907* 71
Postcard of Oslo 88
Rasmus Valentinsen 43
Skippers Sardines label 40
Solheim, Coniston, *1904* (now Gate House) 69
Victorian Manchester 1
Vik church, Sogn 45
Windermere Station, *1907* 85

Our Studio Villa, Balholm, Norway 1907

Introduction

Although many have enjoyed Alfred Heaton Cooper's paintings throughout this century, few people really know much about him; since his death in 1929 hardly a word has been written in his honour or in celebration of his work. Yet Alfred's achievements were considerable. Not only did he found a family dynasty of painters which now runs to three generations, but his own particular, lucid style of landscape painting sold widely in his lifetime and continues to do so. His paintings are instantly recognisable to those who enjoy pictures of the English Lake District, yet the discreet 'A.Heaton Cooper' in the corner gives little away about the painter himself.

Alfred was a modest man, affable and friendly, a dedicated and prolific painter throughout a career which spanned sixty years. He not only painted Lakeland scenery; but from 1905-1929 he also illustrated a popular series of British and European guide books published by A & C Black at a time when travellers relied on colour paintings to serve the same descriptive function that colour photography provides nowadays. His relationship with his public was much the same then as it is today: his work was appreciated by vast numbers of people who never even knew his name. However, this wasn't the case in Norway, where a gallery and a house at Balholm still celebrate his work; he visited the country to paint as a young man, fell in love with it, married and even settled there for a while then continued to visit throughout his life. Although Balholm was also home to a select little band of other European painters, the local people have never forgotten the Englishman, Alfred, who married the dyer's daughter. It is ironic to think that Alfred's name may well be better known in the Fjords than in his native Lancashire.

One reason why no biography has appeared until now is that Alfred was very soon obscured by the growing success of his son, William. After Alfred's death, William had to take his father's place as breadwinner, and his own work started to attract favourable comments and popular recognition. William's particular style of landscape painting and the admiration it quickly won soon eclipsed Alfred's small limelight and as William grew in artistic stature, Alfred almost disappeared from view. The influence that Alfred undoubtedly had on his son, as early teacher and mentor, were never fully recognised - but then William, unlike Alfred, did far more than paint. From early manhood onwards, his paintings have always been a living demonstration of his strong principles and Christian beliefs and painting became a vocation and philosophy of life. William remains Lakeland's single most successful painter in terms of sales, and the demand from his public for a biography resulted in the publication of William's own book about himself, *Mountain Painter*, some years ago.

A second reason was the lack of biographical material. Alfred painted obsessively, tirelessly, and enthusiastically day after day, both outdoors and in his studio. He painted to make a living - failure to produce paintings in sufficient numbers would have meant destitution for his Norwegian wife and their children. This left little time for hobbies and relaxation, and even less for writing anything more than the occasional family letter; consequently he left few papers behind, and even fewer clues about his life, or what he thought about it, where he went and the things that were important and significant to him. This is all very bad news for the biographer - indeed, it made the task of writing about Alfred seem almost impossible.

It was thus hardly surprising that people 'forgot' about Alfred. It was very hard for anyone, however curious, to get to know much about him as a person; and as pleasant a character though he reputedly was, there was little tangible material for a biographer to go on. There were no known family intrigues or scandals, no private papers, no letters stuffed in dusty drawers... just the usual collection of old official documents and a few photographs, and an old trunk full of sketch books - yet it was this shabby old trunk which finally shed light on Alfred`s forgotten past.

There were over a hundred sketch books inside, all meticulously labelled and dated, and by looking at them all carefully, it became possible to see that the books could be 'read' rather than just looked at as picture books. The sketches themselves were intended as ideas for paintings, but their attention to detail went far beyond mere outlines. They reflected life around Alfred, the things that interested him, and the places he visited - drawings which held the key to the whole biography. Alfred, having no time to write, had used his paint brush as a pen and his drawings as words. It soon became clear that to unscramble the information contained in the sketches would provide a fairly accurate record of events in Alfred's life, his commissions and itineraries, his fascinations and frustrations - and once all details had been carefully logged and fed into a computer this is exactly what emerged, becoming a basis on which to construct the biography.

It is the story of a Victorian working class child, whose mother was an illiterate mill worker, but who shared her son's conviction that to paint was the very reason for his existence, and who helped him pursue an art career despite all hardships and disappointments. Painting no doubt also offered the prospect of escape from the humdrum mill town working environment.

It was a very exciting time in which to be a young painter, and the Impressionists and those who adopted the outdoors *en plein air* style influenced Alfred greatly throughout his student days and the years that followed. Life was shared between his two favourite places - Norway and the English Lake District, and he travelled to and fro between the two throughout his life, though frequent book commissions for A & C Black gave him the opportunity of painting in many other locations all over Britain

Alfred Heaton Cooper at Coniston, 1906

and Europe. Despite such an active career, Alfred was never free of the anxiety of money problems, and his life was an endless cycle of painting and selling in order to pay his household bills.

The biography is by no means a comprehensive record of Alfred's life - there are intriguing gaps waiting to be filled, and it would be exciting to think that one day we may discover more... for example, the Bolton school which educated Alfred to such superior standards has yet to be identified, despite extensive enquiries - and there were several painting trips to Europe later in his life about which very little is known. Only one brief diary exists, describing part of a visit to Sweden. It was written on scraps of old paper, but this small fragment of a journal makes it even more frustrating that the rest of it, and others too, may have been lost or not considered worth keeping. Alfred's sharp powers of description are as evident in his prose as they were in his art.

The simple aim of this book is to acknowledge Alfred as the original and innovative landscape painter he was, and to introduce more people to the pleasures of his work. In the Grasmere family studio which still bears his name, thousands of reproductions and dozens of his original paintings are still sold each year. His Victorian style helps to satisfy an apparently insatiable nostalgia and enthusiasm for the bygone romance of the English countryside. It isn't the case that Alfred is 'unknown' - rather that he should be better known.

And so, in answer to all those who have requested to read or know "something about Alfred", this book finally becomes a reality. It was written with true affection for a modest, dedicated and hardworking painter and my only regret is that the acclaim and respect that Alfred's work increasingly attracts should be posthumous.

Jane Renouf

Wrynose Pass and Cockley Beck

Chapter One

"A Boltonian at home"

1863-1884

Records are at variance about the birth date of Alfred Heaton Cooper - according to official documents he was born twice, and in different places. His birth certificate records the date as 14th June 1863 in Swinton, on the outskirts of Manchester, yet a passport issued nearly sixty years later opts for the same day but a year later in Regent Terrace, Halliwell, Bolton. Another passport, six years later, states a third possibility...

Victorian Manchester

Of one thing, at least, there is no doubt - he was born to William and Alice Cooper, both of whom worked in the cotton industry. William was a cashier and Alice a weaver. She could neither read nor write but was to prove the driving force which propelled her children to make the most of what education was available to them and to succeed in careers that few from such a background would have aspired to.

Alfred was the couple's second child; no family documents exist to verify this, but when William, who survived his wife by 28 years, died and was buried in Alice's grave in St Peter's Church, Halliwell, a new headstone was erected which reveals that the grave also held the remains of a little baby called Rachel, born in 1862, who died at the early age of three months.

This infant death must have brought the young couple much sadness at the start of their married life, and one can imagine how precious baby Alfred must have been to them after losing Rachel. It is more than likely that Alice would have turned to her own mother for help and support, and perhaps the Swinton address was where Alice's parents lived, and where Alice returned for her first two confinements.

Alfred was joined very swiftly by a baby brother, John, in 1865 followed by Edith in 1867, and not surprisingly the family moved, probably to a bigger house, in 1867. Thomas was born in 1870, followed by William in 1874 and the family of six children was completed in 1878 by the birth of the baby of the family, Daniel, who was fourteen or fifteen years younger than Alfred. Whether the 1867 move was from Swinton or Halliwell is unclear, but the destination was a house in Markland Hill Lane, situated near Cannon Brothers' Doff Cocker Mill where both William and Alice worked.

Markland Hill today is a suburb of Bolton, high and breezy, its upper boundaries merging with moorland. Although Alfred's family home was demolished a few years ago and the Doff Cocker Mill is long gone, the mill lodge (reservoir) remains and Victorian Markland Hill lies still clearly visible in its winding suburban lanes, wooded slopes and heavy Gothic architecture; Victorian worthies and their families lie under ornate stone angels and obelisks which jostle for space in damp and dripping churchyards just as they did in Alfred's young day, and despite the addition of motor traffic and lines of pre-war semis, Alfred would have little difficulty finding his way round his homeground today.

The Coopers' house in Markland Hill Lane, 1975 (now demolished)

Local newspaper reports about Alfred in later, more famous years, insisted that William and Alice were so ambitious for their young son, they scrimped and saved to send him to be "privately" educated, from the age of four. However hard they worked, it is difficult to imagine cotton mill wages affording such privilege, nor where it would be available near Markland Hill. Alfred's son, the painter William Heaton Cooper, whose personal memories have brought such richness of colour to the sketchy outlines of his father's life history throughout this book, agreed a private education sounds improbable:

"With two hard-working parents and six children, I think its very unlikely. I think he'd just go to the local primary school and secondary school, whatever it was in those days," he said.

Could "private" school have meant a dame's establishment, from which Alfred would have emerged to continue his education at a secondary school? Despite extensive searches and long hours poring over school registers and directories for the period, there is no record at any local schools of any of the Cooper children as pupils on the school role.

This is especially disappointing; for whatever educational body was responsible for teaching the six children, whether it was an elementary board school, Bolton Grammar School or one of several church schools in the vicinity, the education must have been remarkably inspiring, leaving all the Heaton Cooper children with ambitions and aspirations which took them all far beyond their Markland Hill environment. Art, in particular, must have been held in high regard. Not only did Alfred aspire to be, and eventually become an artist but a similar education produced an art career for Thomas which culminated in his appointment as a Master of Painting at Cleveland School of Art, Ohio, where he wrote an important book on perspective, while Daniel's art led him into photography and emigration to Boston, USA, where he became a well known and much respected photographer. Alfred himself was instrumental in furthering his youngest brother's career. According to William:

"Daniel was a very good photographer but he hadn't much of a business sense, but my father had. He was very good at helping his younger brothers into things that they should have been doing, and so he introduced Daniel to a newspaper man in Bolton and this man gave him a job. Well, eventually, he went to Boston and did very well and became one of the best photographers in Boston."

Although very little is actually known about the children's mother, Alice, William was certain that it was his grandmother's influence which paved the way to his father's career as an artist. She was admired for her strength of character and determination, and her great feeling for art:

"She was a natural, she just had this thing art in her - it's very mysterious, some people have it and some don't. We never met our grandmother, we were very sorry to miss her. Alfred was fond of his father - but although he had his father's broad brow, he didn't have what was going on inside it! He was fond of him, but not as much as of his mother. She was the one that really guided the family from their birth."

Alice worked hard as a weaver in the cotton mill to provide for her family, and if any of the children ever did teach her to read and write, she wrote nothing that was kept for posterity. The only mark that can be attributed to her at all was an 'X' which represented her signature on her marriage vows and on Alfred's birth certificate.

Alfred left school at 14 to follow in the safety and security of his father's footsteps into an office job. His father must have been delighted at his choice, guaranteeing as it did financial security and social position. The job was as a junior accountancy clerk at Bolton Town Hall in various departments including the Waterworks, and his salary, however small, must have helped to keep all his little brothers and sister at home and in their various schools.

If Alfred was accomplished as a clerk with his figures, meticulous, neat and accurate, little was said about it. He was, however, remembered for the excellence of his copperplate hand, which was held up as an example to other junior clerks. Undoubtedly, his basic grounding in book-keeping was a most valuable skill to acquire, and one which he used throughout his life to record his sales and to try and keep the family finances in credit as he struggled to earn a living as an artist.

Despite his father's obvious approval and encouragement of a career in

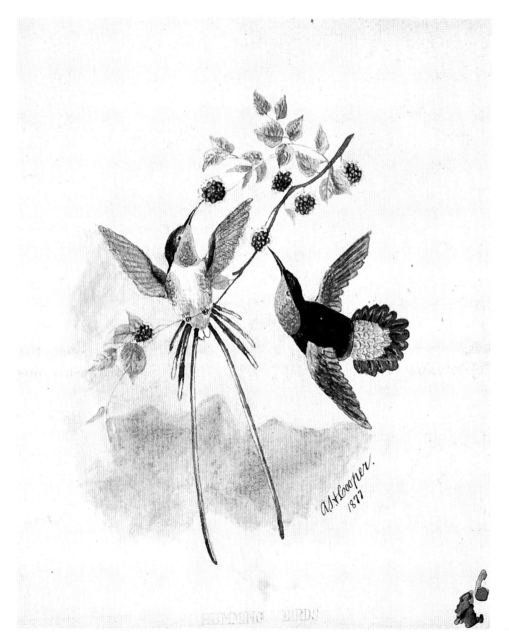

Humming Birds 1877

local government bureaucracy, Alfred's heart was not in it, and his mind certainly wandered off it. The interest which he had enjoyed in art and drawing at school continued to grow, and even the clouds scudding by the window outside Bolton Town Hall were too much of a temptation to be resisted as Alfred's hand would go to his waistcoat pocket, to reach the small sketch book which he carried everywhere and a simple skyscape would emerge, his columns of figures forgotten for the moment. His free time was spent wandering the moors and visiting local beauty spots near Markland Hill to sketch. His mother was delighted with his efforts and encouraged Alfred to take private lessons, for which she paid by taking extra weaving at the mill.

A few of these very earliest examples of Alfred's work still exist, including a neatly copied work, painted very delicately in water colours entitled *Humming Birds, A. H. Cooper, 1877*. The lightness of his touch and the depth of tiny detail achieved by Alfred at only fourteen years old is still quite stunning to look at and indicates the influence that important painters like John Ruskin were already having on the eager young Alfred.

These early paintings continue to delight with their young freshness. His artist son, William, assessed them over a century later with his own special wisdom and experience:

"There are some paintings of his that we sometimes come across, we have one now of these little streams that come trickling down from the moors out of the heather, and then you get down into the ash trees and the oak trees and willows - and they're very nice, pure first hand observation, too, nothing traditional about them, Alfred was experiencing the beauty of nature in these pure, first hand efforts."

Alfred's first numbered sketch book is inscribed in his copperplate *Alf'd H. Cooper, Oct 1879, No. 1* and is dedicated almost entirely to copying William Turner drawings.

The influence that the great man had on Alfred extended beyond mere admiration of Turner's magnificent mastery of romantic landscape painting; it is quite clear from Alfred's sketch books that he actually walked in the Master's footsteps, choosing to paint many of the places that Turner visited during his well-documented tour of the hills and dales of Northern England in 1816.

Turner had been commissioned by Longmans to produce 120 watercolours, at a fee of three thousand guineas, to illustrate seven volumes of a work entitled *Grand History of the County of York*. The story of that journey, and the paintings which resulted, has been told in entertaining detail in a book by David Hill (*In Turner's Footsteps*, published by Book Club Associates, 1984). It cannot have been co-incidence that, seventy-five years later, Alfred started to visit almost every one of Turner's locations. Some were, of course, famous beauty spots or landmarks, like Aysgarth Falls, or

Alfred's sketch from an etching by Turner in Ruskin's "Works" Vol V

Hornby; but what of Mitton, Ribblesdale; or Dallam Tower at Milnthorpe; or *Where Tees and Greta Meet*, near Rokesby? This dogged pursuit of Turner must have been intentional and a valuable learning experience.

The power of Turner`s work, which inspired Alfred over several years to seek out his viewpoints, remains as compulsive today. When writing *In Turners's Footsteps*, David Hill not only traced each stopping place on the journey; he also travelled the very same route on the same days of the month as Turner had done.

Alfred didn't go quite as far as that in seeking to discover the essential Turner. His journeys had to be done when he could afford the time and the

Study of boats at Lymm

All among the barley

All among the barley - as Comin' through the Rye.

fare and following in Turner's footsteps was something he enjoyed over a period of about three years, starting at the very beginning of his painting career. The sketches and paintings which resulted were original and very different from Turner's work. Alfred introduced far more careful detail, with less reliance on mood and effect to create an impression. Compared with Turner, Alfred's work lacked the excitement and panache of the romanticist; instead it showed the shape and texture of nature, unobscured by a golden mist or a sweeping storm.

Alfred's interest in Turner began in the way that a pupil might be

Peace - after J. Ruskin "Modern Painter"

84 Peace. after J Ruskin. "Modern Painter"

interested in his teacher's technique. A simple pencil sketch of two trees is inscribed with some reverence by Alfred: *Two Scotch Firs in Turner's etching of Inverary. In perfect poise, representing a double action, the warping of the trees away from the sea wind and the continual growing out of boughs on the right hand side to recover the balance.*

There are also pollarded willows copied from Turner's etching of *The Young Anglers*, and a scene from the River Loire by Turner, reproduced by Ruskin in *Modern Painters*. Alfred copied Ruskin, too. He once sketched an Italianate walled town and entrance gate in the style of Ruskin himself, entitled *Peace - after J. Ruskin*.

But by the time Alfred began his second sketch book, just a year or so later, he was ready to venture out into his own style, albeit under the guidance of Tristram Ellis, whose advice and instructions taken from *Sketching From Nature* were important enough for Alfred to quote in the front cover of the sketch book. He copied out:

Make small sketches, about 6" by 4" as quickly as you can, without attempting any detail, but carefully noting the <u>values</u> and <u>colours</u>. These are called '<u>impressions</u>' and should be made in great numbers by all landscape artists, it is only thus they can get a true appreciation of <u>natural</u> colour and tone. Their work, after a course of them, will acquire a <u>solidity</u> and strength that it had no trace of before. <u>Values</u> are the only means of <u>correctly representing effects</u>.

The water colour sketches which follow illustrate bold strides forward in the development of Alfred's painting technique, which left his books and copying behind and took him instead to face the world of landscape for himself. At sixteen years old, Alfred was finally able to achieve a small measure of independence which allowed him to travel far more freely, and

Halliwell Glen, 1883

with the help of the train, he reached painting destinations like Dallam Tower, Milnthorpe; Heysham and Silverdale in Lancashire; Haweswater in Westmorland and Delamere Forest in Cheshire. Following Tristam Ellis's guidance, Alfred worked swiftly to produce his impressions, often writing in details of tone and colour which could be added to complete the work at a later date.

By the early 1880s, art had become so important in Alfred's life that both he and his mother recognised that his talent warranted not only proper training and tuition, but a full-time career as an artist, leaving the Town Hall and its safe respectability behind. Risking his father's disapproval, Alfred and his mother decided to send some of his work to London to try and secure a place at art college for Alfred. According to William:

"Alice persuaded her husband to let him go from the Town Hall job, but I think there was a sort of plot with Alfred and his mother to find out about this and to send some drawings as an example. So they did this without

telling my grandfather; and my grandmother was so good at persuading William to let him go, and William wasn't anything like powerful enough to stop him going!"

The portfolio he submitted of watercolours painted at Borrowdale not only secured a place to study, but even provided free tuition for Alfred to become an art student for three years, starting at the age of 21.

But Alice and Alfred's undoubted delight at this success was tragically short-lived. Mother and son were separated forever on January 29th, 1883, when Alice died.

The cause of Alice's death at forty years old is not known. Suffice to say she had mothered seven children in twenty years, working throughout this time in the mill to ensure her children's futures, and had taken little rest or reward for herself over the years. Her husband, William, was devastated by Alice's death and became withdrawn and silent until his own death twenty-eight years later in 1911:

"He was a small man, very shy and nervous of meeting people. He stayed with us twice after his wife died and I think he must have rather given up the adventure of living. He just sat there and said nothing most of the time", his grandson William remembered.

Alfred's decision to leave Bolton Town Hall, forsake his income and head for London and the unknown must have been particularly hard to stick to after his mother's death. Not only was her loving support and encouragement gone forever, but his departure from home meant less help for his father and the older children in caring for the younger ones. Edith was 17 by this time, and would have been expected to take her mother's place in caring for the family. Daniel, the youngest child, was still only seven, and the responsibility on the older children must have been a heavy one, especially in view of William's solemnity and silent grief.

Though Alice's death robbed Alfred of the joy and excitement of his venture, he decided, despite this setback, to pursue his new career. Perhaps her untimely death made it even more vital for him to prove that Alice's pride and confidence in his artistic ability had not been misplaced. He left Markland Hill for London in the autumn of 1884 to become an artist.

Abridged Family Tree

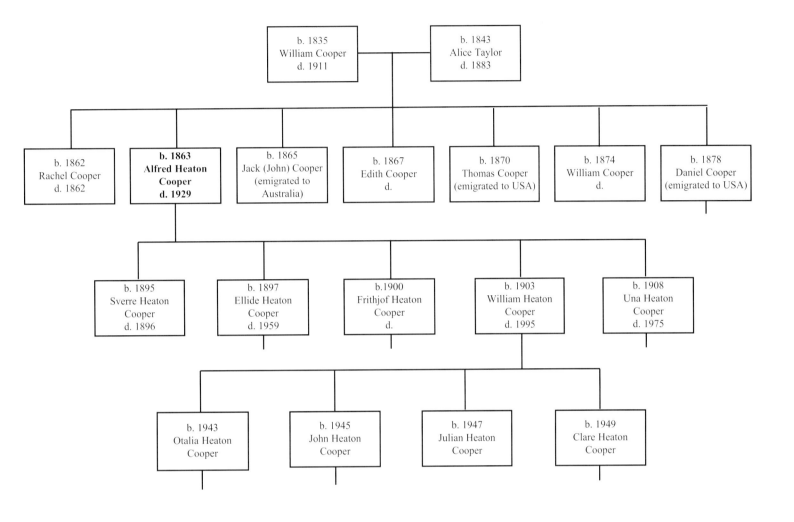

b. 1835
William Cooper
d. 1911

b. 1843
Alice Taylor
d. 1883

b. 1862
Rachel Cooper
d. 1862

b. 1863
Alfred Heaton
Cooper
d. 1929

b. 1865
Jack (John) Cooper
(emigrated to
Australia)

b. 1867
Edith Cooper
d.

b. 1870
Thomas Cooper
(emigrated to USA)

b. 1874
William Cooper
d.

b. 1878
Daniel Cooper
(emigrated to USA)

b. 1895
Sverre Heaton
Cooper
d. 1896

b. 1897
Ellide Heaton
Cooper
d. 1959

b.1900
Frithjof Heaton
Cooper
d.

b. 1903
William Heaton
Cooper
d. 1995

b. 1908
Una Heaton
Cooper
d. 1975

b. 1943
Otalia Heaton
Cooper

b. 1945
John Heaton
Cooper

b. 1947
Julian Heaton
Cooper

b. 1949
Clare Heaton
Cooper

A.H.Cooper. 1885.

Haymaking near Chorley

Chapter Two

London, a student of life and art

1884-1889

Alfred Heaton Cooper as a young man, 1885

Student drawings

Art colleges in the 1880s anywhere in Europe must have been exciting places to be; and Alfred's years as an art student happened to co-incide with one of the most active periods of challenge and change in Western European art. Nothing was left unquestioned. Motives, technique, style and meaning were endlessly analysed, and the role of the artist himself in relation to society became almost as hotly debated as the relative merits of Naturalism compared with Classicism or Romanticism.

It is impossible to review Alfred's student days in London without first examining some of the things that he learned and subsequently allowed to influence his own painting. The exciting developments within popular art during the previous sixty years gave Alfred's tutors plenty of subject matter to fascinate their students, and by recalling those developments, it is possible to understand more clearly how Alfred himself arrived at his own style of painting.

Alfred's dilemma whether to be a painter or an accountancy clerk was, in itself, a new problem in a new age. Gone were the days when painting or sculpture was handed down from father to son as a craft. For the past century, painters had been busy arguing that art required intellect and intelligence and was a cerebral activity. Artists and craftsmen were more than skilled labourers in an ordinary trade - they were thinkers and philosophers too. And if painting was an intellectual activity, then it could be taught like any other subject, they argued. People with no family tradition of art could go to a college and learn how to paint just as students of medicine acquired the knowledge to become doctors. Artistry could be acquired by education rather than simply inherited.

Thus the choice Alfred made, to learn art as an educational subject in a college was quite a new and modern choice. The fact that nobody in his family could pass on to him the skills of painting as part of a traditional cottage industry did not prevent him from following his natural instinct to paint, as indeed it might have done if he had been born in the century before.

Alfred's vital decision to be a painter was only the first of many choices he had to make as an artist in this prolific and progressive period. It had only been within the past sixty years that landscape painting began to reflect what the human eye actually saw rather than a classical or even imaginary composition of neo-Greek or Roman symmetry.

More radical even than that was the painter's departure from his studio, where all his work had formerly been executed in colours that were deemed correct for the subject, however inaccurate. Suddenly, in the 1800s, painters emerged from indoors blinking in the bright light of day, where they set up easels out of doors and began to work in the open air. Suddenly grass was no longer a dingy brown, as artists had been required to paint it. Thanks to Constable's pursuit of truth, green grass was painted green, despite the storm of criticism which followed such innovation.

JMW Turner had been Alfred's greatest influence in pre-student days. He copied Turner's sketches and drawings fervently in his own notebook, and even wrote out quotations from Turner's own notes. For Turner, painting a landscape was like making a statement about nature; his extrovert work preached the grandeur and majesty of nature, his painting expressed his own emotions as he looked on at a stormy sea or vivid sunset. The paintings are vibrant with the romance and splendour of nature as Turner perceived it, and he often let the overall effect of power and pageantry overwhelm the small details which were lost in swirling spray or mist.

What a contrast with the unoriginal contrivances of classical composition which had passed as landscape paintings just a few decades before! The teenage Alfred was evidently impressed and when he then discovered Constable a little later as a student, he was equally influenced. In fact, Alfred's own paintings reflect more of Constable's quest for simple realism and the truth than they owe to Turner's dashing romanticism. But Alfred's own style, slowly emerging like a butterfly from a chrysalis, always avoided plagiarism and favoured instead a clever

Lakeland waterfall

technique of adaptation. Alfred managed to incorporate rather than copy so that his work never lacked originality.

Forecasters at the London Weather Centre say it must have rained later in the afternoon that Constable's hay wain trundled through the ford at Dedham Mill - the detail with which he painted his wide sky made it quite possible to forecast the weather that lay ahead. This is even more remarkable than it might seem when one remembers that Constable generally only sketched outside. He returned to his studio to paint.

It was Constable's very struggle to reproduce nature exactly as his eye perceived it which encouraged the group of French artists known as the Barbizon School to pursue his ideal and add more muscle to the revolution in painting which was gradually evolving. Although the Barbizon adherents had first met in 1848, almost forty years before Alfred learnt about them, he admired their initiative in taking painting even further away from the studio than Constable had dared and he considered their ideals still worth emulating, half a century later.

From the work of the Barbizon School, and the three painters that Alfred was known to admire greatly, namely Diez, Rousseau and Eugene Boudin, came Impressionism, whose ideal was to convey the momentary aspect of things seen. The term Impressionist was first applied to the paintings these innovative artists exhibited at a small Parisian gallery, and far from being complimentary, the word was first used in derision. However, Impressionists brought a new vision to art, which soon became popular and admired. They painted exactly what they saw, concentrating on the effects of light and atmosphere; and if a shadow made the grass look purple, they painted it purple.

But the new quest for realism extended beyond landscape to people, and for the first time, pictures began to feature ordinary people doing ordinary things. Millet's scenes from peasant life which recorded people working at mundane tasks are echoed years later in Alfred's numerous studies of peasants in Norway going about their everyday lives, or the charcoal burners and woodmen of Hawkshead or Oxenfell. Millet lent respectability and dignity to the painting of the common man; prior to the nineteenth century, only the rich and famous featured in paintings, the portraits commissioned to influence or flatter. But Millet's realistic depiction of a reaper working in a field helped to change public perception of what constituted art and was worthy of painting, and his influence, together with that of the many artists who began to paint in a similar vein, inspired Alfred to seek out and paint ordinary people at work in such detail that these drawings and paintings are as valuable as records of social history as they are works of art.

Throughout his life, Alfred painted water in the form of lakes, streams, rivers and seascapes. Painting water in flow intrigued him, as did the

The Night Train to Blackpool, 1895

movement of the sea, and he admired the work of a Norwegian painter living in Paris by the name of Fritz Towlow.

"This man influenced my father greatly", William remembered. *"He was an extremely fine painter of water, rivers, torrents - and snow laden banks with trees growing out of them... but especially the movement of water. I can see traces of that influence in my father's work."*

And how better to learn to paint water, and to do so entirely out of doors, than to combine the two by the simple expedient of living afloat on a boat or barge, which allowed *en plein air* actuality and realism to be practised comfortably on board. Monet and his friends may have done it first, but the idea appealed to Alfred; and the delightful way in which he took to the water himself as a student painter will be recounted later.

When the Impressionists abandoned the artificiality of the studio and went out into the bright summer light, they discovered that when the human eye looks at a particular scene in nature, it sees a mass of colour rather than single things in particular colours. Monet took painting out of doors even

Charcoal Burners at Bouth 1908

further by decreeing that all paintings should be started and completed entirely *en plein air* and to comply with this new requirement for naturalism, his admirers dashed off brief but complete paintings in the space of a morning, or a day at the most.

Impressionism marched boldly on; soon, the creation of light and atmosphere was enough to be a painting, but even its most dedicated practitioners realised it needed developing further before they could, as Cezanne put it, *"turn Impressionism into something more solid and enduring, like the art of museums."* His work, in particular, gave landscape depth and more solidity and encouraged others to experiment within the spectrum of Impressionism, as Seurat did with Pointillism.

Almost every major development in nineteenth century art not only left its mark on Alfred, but became a part of his own style, adapted, re-moulded and eventually grafted on to his own to make him a unique and original painter. The way he used others' art was very similar to the way in which George Clausen had developed his own style. Clausen was eleven years older than Alfred. He became an RA at an early age and had a popular and successful London art career. The two men met while Alfred was studying in London and it is thought that Clausen actually taught the young Alfred. Not

The Reapers

surprising, then, that Clausen, who studied, selected and incorporated the very best of 19th century art into his own, should have taught Alfred to do the same. Those contemporaries who wrote about Clausen at the time praised him for the way in which he allowed the shadows of Constable, Turner and Millet to lurk quietly and skilfully in his own work. Clausen was popular and well thought of throughout his life, and Alfred undoubtedly benefited from their acquaintance.

Not a day of learning was wasted as Clausen and others helped Alfred to explore the work of all the famous names and learn to weave their ideas into his own. Turner's drama and passion occasionally inspired a romantic flourish in Alfred's skies, while Constable's meticulous realism prompted Alfred to be almost photographically exact in his landscapes. Alfred may well have agreed with those who summed up Impressionism as little more than "witty improvisation". But the idea of painting almost entirely *en plein air* as the Barbizons insisted, was so attractive to Alfred that he adopted it throughout his life, though his work was far too detailed and solid in form to be labelled as Impressionist; it would be more accurate to call it Impressionist-influenced - and he had no interest whatsoever in post-Impressionism.

Without his art education and the influences that became part of his own style, would Alfred's work have progressed beyond the "pure first hand observation" of his boyhood days if he had never travelled beyond Bolton?

Attending classes at both the Royal Institute of Art, and Westminster School, where Alfred went for his life classes certainly involved a degree of book-learning to familiarise students with the history of art. For Alfred, though, art was drawing and painting, rather than reading about others doing it.

The Stone Pickers by George Clausen, 1887

Theatre Royal, Drury Lane,
before and after the fire, 1884

One of his first student digs in 1884 was at 72, Cheyne Walk, Chelsea, in a quaint and narrow old house sandwiched between two taller buildings. His rooms were above the business premises of E. MAUNDER, who may have had a greengrocery shop if Alfred's own 1886 sketch of the building is accurate. A sloping display stand, probably for fruit and vegetables, is pushed against the shop window, and a lady is taking her small dog for a walk past the shop. The vital clue that this house was Alfred's digs lies in the address at the front of this early sketch book. His useful and methodical habit of writing his name, address and the date helps to clarify many details about his life which would otherwise have been unrecorded and uncheckable.

Alfred appears to have started his life in London at 84, Cadogan Place before moving to Cheyne Walk between autumn 1884, when his studies started, and the following March, when his address changed to 6, Upper Cheyne Row, Chelsea. One of his first student assignments was to sketch the trees in Hyde Park. His work reveals a very rural Hyde Park with clumps of silver birch and extraordinarily old and gnarled species of arboreal antiquity. These trees gave Alfred plenty of scope for studies in shape and texture.

During these first months at college, his sketchbooks provide historic little vignettes of London life: the sheep grazing in Battersea Park; an incongruously lush green growth of cactus, also in Battersea Park; a visit to South Kensington Museum to sketch a Greco-Roman mask; sailing ships on the Thames at Chelsea Bridge and barges seen from the Embankment; and a wet evening in Annet Street, Pimlico Wharf.

A small mystery surrounds Alfred's apparent fascination for sketching the Theatre Royal during these months. A portrait entitled *The Commissionaire* appeared in his current sketch book, dated October 20 1884, followed by drawings of the frontage of a Victorian theatre or music hall, perhaps the Theatre Royal, Drury Lane. However, it looks as though catastrophe struck the building; for in the next sketches it appears to be reduced to charred wreckage, the remains of its grand columns no longer holding up the balconies above, but exposed to the sky. The regal staircase remains weirdly in place, but its stairs lead nowhere as firemen still aim hoses at the smoking ruins. The way in which the fire had eaten away at the ornate balustrade and staircase fascinated Alfred so much that he went closer to sketch it in detail, perhaps at some risk to life and limb. The big fire devastated the grand building, wherever it was; but its whereabouts cannot have been far away from Cheyne Walk, or Alfred would not have had time to record the fire on the spot.

In June Alfred returned home to Markland Hill for the summer vacation, during which he sketched studiously in the hay fields and copses of Whaley Bridge, Horwich Moors and Ribblesdale, drawing sheep and cows, hens and cockerel, oak, sycamore, and elm trees. His delicate pencil details of honeysuckle and wild roses in July 1885 would have done justice to any Victorian lady's Nature Notes, and how fascinating if Alfred had revealed the name of the model who posed for *Meditation* a month earlier on June 17, 1885. A young woman, sad and sombre, eyes closed, casts a shadow on the wall behind her. Could this possibly have been Alfred's young sister, Edith, her mother so recently dead and the burdens of caring for the family heavy on her shoulders? The simple drawing is blurred and softened, the artist's eye compassionate.

Back in London again, by far the greatest attraction to the young artist during his student days was the river and its boats. Throughout the autumn before, especially in November 1884, he had walked in Monet's footsteps some thirteen years after the French Impressionist had painted *On Westminster Bridge*, visiting haunts up and down the Thames including Mortlake, the Pool of London and Greenwich. His work, so reminiscent of Monet, and so similar to Monet's later Thames paintings of the early 1900s, shows the lively river awash with merchant vessels; tug boats chug around the big sailing vessels, rowing boats and punts provide useful foregrounds to his busy riverscapes. The life of the river obviously excited him, and in the spring of 1886, he ventured further afield up the Thames to Old Windsor, where he found an old wooden shed

Annet Street, Pimlico - evening study in black and white, 1884

Cactus in Battersea Park

Alfred's digs at Cheyne Walk, 1886

Meditation

in a riverside garden near Haines' Ferry, which he rented and converted into a studio.

The idea of the garden studio was a popular one for artists at that time. Reared on "plein airism" and natural realism, where better to find it than down the garden? Wealthy artists with large country houses built decorative, ornate little studios in the grounds. Alfred's equivalent was a garden shed in an overgrown field. The shed had a sloping roof, a big wide window and a skylight window in the roof propped open with a pole. Bitterly cold in winter, stuffy in summer but in all probability Alfred would hardly have noticed. From student painter he had finally graduated to studio artist.

Exciting as the city had been, Alfred was known to have disliked the crowds and noise and he had felt closed in and claustrophobic living in London, even somewhere as relatively pleasant as Chelsea. Windsor brought him back to nature and fresh air, though living so far out inevitably distanced him from his college and contributed to his decision later to leave without finishing his studies, preferring to paint rather than learn more about painting.

We know that the little shed at Old Windsor had rush matting on the floor, and the Thames ran slowly by, just a few feet beyond the shed door, which opened inwards. No verbal description could rival Alfred's detailed ink sketch of his simple studio. Even the date on his calendar is visible; it was Saturday November 6th as he worked, and the work was finished four days later, according to Alfred's inscription at the bottom, which reads: *Corner bit of Studio - Old Windsor - looking over Thames, 10th Nov '86.*

It seems likely that he lived and painted in the same small space. A narrow couch or chaise longue, with Alfred's stylish but well worn shoes kicked casually underneath indicate that the studio had to double as living accommodation. His straw boater and jacket hang by the open door, his walking stick and umbrella rest on nails below, and a large parasol stands furled behind the door. His clay pipe leans against a tobacco pouch beside the oil lamp on the table, behind which rests a large canvas, draped over with a fringed shawl or towel.

But it is the wall and its homely additions which provide the best details of Alfred's life and tastes. He worked with such minute perfection that even a letter lying casually on the narrow shelf reveals his own name above the address, when examined under a magnifying glass. An unfinished sketch of a riverscene is pinned to a board and left propped on the shelf for future completion, and a decorative poster, labelled *"Paris Artiste"* perhaps advertised a Parisian exhibition or had been the front cover of a popular magazine of the time. Above it is pinned a drawing or painting of a woman labouring in the fields, carrying a bundle of corn on her shoulders, much in the style of Millet's *Reapers*; was it something original Alfred had done, or his own copy from a painting he particularly he admired?

Other small works are pinned close by, above the clothes brush on the shelf and to the right of the mirror which hangs on a hook. Taking centre place in Alfred's display is the back view of a nude lady, who cavorts across the picture, buxom and carefree, and the minute lettering just visible under magnification reads: *Md BONSITEFLAU.* A hat box, two small portmanteaux and a portfolio are stacked against the wall, and a spray of teasel decorates the space above the door. A curious, tent-like canopy seems to be suspended from the ceiling and secured to the wall, but whether it improved the light, kept the draughts out or added a touch of the exotic to this garden shed is unclear.

No photograph could have better captured the tiny detail that Alfred so lovingly and painstakingly included. Looking at the picture one hundred years later, it almost feels as if Alfred himself had invited the observer to take a privileged glimpse into his personal and domestic life; but instead of looking inwards at the small room, the observer stands beside Alfred on the rush matting looking out at the river landscape through his eyes.

Near Haines' Garden, which was close by the studio shed, was Haines' Ferry, and a little further up stood the famous old riverside inn, the *Bells of Ouzeley*, where Alfred repaired one wet day in April 1886 to sketch his fellow drinkers. The inn was roughly furnished with tables but no chairs, and drinkers clad in capes, looking uncommonly like Hansom cabbies, stand by the tables looking out on a sailing boat passing on the river. By contrast, *On The Datchet Road, nr Windsor*, speaks of Victorian suburban gentility in the neat row of villas which could easily still be standing today. How Alfred must have enjoyed the tranquility of sketching along the riverbank or the quiet, clean streets of Old Windsor after the bustle of life in London.

Not far from his studio, he visited Manor Farm, Old

Sheep in Battersea Park 1886

Wet day in the "Bells of Ouzeley", 1886

Alfred's studio by the Thames at Old Windsor, 1886

Windsor, where a 150-year-old statue of a seal in the grounds fascinated Alfred enough to sketch from both front and back; more interesting by far than the seal is the casual silhouette of Windsor Castle which dominates the background. With such historic, Royal architecture lying so near to his humble studio, it is amazing that Alfred never appears to have attempted any drawings or paintings of the Castle, preferring, instead, to sketch the willows at Wraysbury or Magna Carta Island.

In August, 1887, Alfred took a summer holiday. The popularity of boating was already established, and only two years later, in 1889, Jerome K. Jerome's *Three Men In A Boat*, proved such a best-seller, it soon became a classic which tickled the national sense of humour and appealed to popular sentiment. Jerome's book was based on the sort of watery escapade that young gentlemen or students like Alfred would have indulged in. Perhaps Jerome was sitting on the river bank that warm August in 1887 as he searched for inspiration and found it when he saw Alfred and his friends drift by.

But Alfred's slow meanderings upstream with friends on the Thames from August 12th 1887 until September 1st was far more than jolly student japes. No doubt there was plenty of innocent fun as Alfred and friends rowed up from Windsor to Abingdon and back, camping on the riverbank each night. The importance of the trip to all who know and admire Alfred's work is his pictorial diary of the journey, and the versatility that encouraged him to work for the first time with pen and ink. (Oils would have been too slow and inconvenient to use on the little boat). He sketched not only riverscapes, but life in the quiet and picturesque villages he discovered.

If he subsequently painted in more detail from the sketches he penned, the paintings could not have been more delicate or charming than his original penwork. The first drawing is unconnected with the journey, and labelled simply *Going To The Bath* - a barefoot little country girl of perhaps seven or eight years old smiles with mischief as she walks down steps to the riverbank clutching a puppy which is about to be doused in the cold water. If Alfred had ever forsaken landscape art for popular portraiture in the style of *Going To The Bath* his work would certainly have rivalled *Bubbles* in its appeal to Victorian sentiment.

The first stopping place from Old Windsor was Bray where Alfred sketched the church from his boat on the river, and then went ashore to concentrate on details of village cottages.

On the Datchet Road, near Windsor, 1886

Going to the Bath, 1887

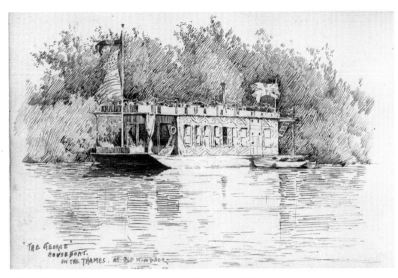

"The George", houseboat on the Thames, 1887

From Bray, on August 12th, the party reached Cliveden Woods, where they camped up a small backwater. At Shiplake it was an enormous tree on an island in the river which Alfred thought worthy of sketching, and on August 16th he stopped at Whitchurch to draw a Tudor house on the opposite bank. This drawing was intended to become an oil painting at a later date because Alfred went to great trouble to note the details of the colours he would need to use - *"greeny grey umbery in shade of walls of house, yellower and lighter greys in lighter walls..."* Perhaps a painting emerged from this fine sketch sometime later, perhaps not; but whatever the final outcome, Alfred obviously thought little of his "rough" drawing. His scribbled outline of reeds and ducks in pencil at the bottom left-hand corner of the river and the quotation *Where the duck dabbles 'neath the rustling sedge - Wordsworth*, effectively vandalise the delicate drawing. Its value to him was obviously no more than a guide to the painting which would follow.

"Cliveden Woods from the backwater where we camped", 1887

On August 21st, the boat reached the wide reaches by Abingdon, and two days later, Alfred sat in Dorchester Churchyard to draw the old cross and porch. The friends must have moored at Dorchester for a day or so, leaving Alfred time to record Dorchester's ancient thatched cottages and an old well surrounded with bucket, bowl and kettle. On August 26th they passed under Shillingford Bridge close by Wittenham Clumps in the early morning, leaving time for Alfred to spend the day in Benson, where another child provided him with a subject for a country portrait. A lad of about fourteen quite smartly dressed in a jacket with collar and tie, knickerbockers, stockings and shoes with buckles looks at Alfred with a self-conscious grin as he carries a heavy basket down the road. Behind him there are more thatched cottages with roses growing up the walls, so different from the rows of terraced back-to-backs and the grey, weather-beaten slate of Alfred's native Bolton.

By August 29th, the boat had returned back downstream as far as Goring, where the Old Mill provided an excellent subject to draw, with its weirdly shaped pollarded willows so attractive to Alfred, who shared Turner's fascination for drawing them. Passing another tranquil old mill at Streatley, they camped at Streatley Hill near Pangbourne on August 30th, where it rained, and after a brief sketch of Cookham Church Tower on September 1st, there is nothing more to plot the holiday until Alfred returned to Old Windsor and drew a magnificent houseboat called *The George* which was moored there.

This series of drawings may only ever have been intended as rough guides to the paintings Alfred eventually hoped to complete, but the subtlety of his shading and the architectural detail he was capable of copying so minutely with his thin nib make it regrettable that Alfred abandoned pen work after this early stage of his career.

Alfred's progress up the Thames marked the end of his student days and life in London and Old Windsor. The following spring he abandoned them both in search of brighter sunshine and a touch of exotica, and embarked on the *SS Malta* on April 4th to sail to Tangier via Gibraltar.

The crossing by the Bay of Biscay and down the coast of Spain was gentle enough to allow Alfred to sit on the deck making pen sketches of the ship and his fellow passengers. When the ship passed by the Rock of Gibraltar, and Apes Hill, it was greeted by a shoal of porpoises, and when *Malta* arrived at Tangier, Alfred booked himself into the Hotel Central until June 14th, which gave him five weeks to devote to Moorish architecture and everyday life in the kasbah.

His sketches during this entire trip were done in pen and ink, and were similar in detail and delicacy to those of his Thames holiday the summer before. Despite the care he took sketching, these particular drawings were only ever intended to form the basis of the paintings which developed from them. Some of them are nothing short of miniature masterpieces which deserve far wider appraisal than they ever found, tucked away and forgotten for years between the pages of his sketch books. His first effort in Tangier was dated April 9, 1888, and concentrated on *Tangier housetops - Moorish.*

Old Well at Dorchester, 1887

Benson Village, near Oxford, 1887

On board "SS Malta" 1888

Alfred, ever the realist, also included the Moorish family washing strung up across his housetops.

Soon Alfred progressed from rooftops to people, and on April 11th he went to the souk, or Soko as he called it, to sketch Arabs going about their business. Alfred was a tall, commanding figure of a man; and it is quite noticeable that the Moroccan Arabs hurrying by in their djellabahs seemed very small by comparison to the artist who exaggerated this contrast with himself by drawing them in as very small, almost stunted figures.

The Hotel Central according to Alfred's sketch, appeared to be at the top of a cliff, overlooking both the town and the beach. His delight in recording

27

The Old Souk, Tangiers, 1888

fine detail with his pen was admirably suited to the architectural intricacies of Moorish mosques, no better example of this being his drawings of the tower of the *Mosque of The Prophet* and the doorway of the *Mosque El Kebir*. But it was, for once, the human figure which fascinated him most, and whatever the scene, it was rarely without at least three or four small Arab figures placed importantly in the foreground.

At the beginning of May, he ventured out of Tangier to look at village life, and met some Timbuctoo minstrels. Along the Spartel road he stopped to draw Arab peasant houses, which were single storey huts with thatched roofs. Back in Tangier he looked once again at these small people; *A Moor of Tangier* enveloped by his wide robes and brandishing a wooden staff looks so dwarf-like that the tall Alfred could almost have been exaggerating the man`s diminutive stature.

On June 13th, Alfred left Tangier for Gibraltar where he spent a week staying at the Hotel Calpe before sailing for home.

But where was home during the following autumn and winter? Was it Windsor or Markland Hill? It is not possible to tell - there are no sketch books in the family's collection to take us from June 1888 until April 1889. It is inconceivable that Alfred did no drawing or painting during this time, so the only conclusion that can be reached is that they are lost.

Hotel Central, Tangiers, 1888

Soko Gate, Tangier, 1888

In all likelihood, Alfred would have gone home to Markland Hill to see if it was possible for him to earn a living by his painting. Although based near Bolton, Alfred travelled as extensively as he had before going to London, and one of the places he would almost certainly have headed for was the Mersey estuary.

Two of his first known seascapes, dated 1885, were painted while on holiday from art college. One is of a merchantman sailing ship, the other of an armed sailing vessel with gun ports, both pictured in the Mersey channel. Much of Alfred's work during this early period, including these two paintings, was framed and hung by the art dealers Thomas Bromley's of Bradshawgate, Bolton. Alfred's love of the sea earned him his first Royal Academy showing in 1887 when *Bad News From The Cape* was selected for the summer exhibition, and in all probability, Alfred would have headed back to the estuary occasionally during the summer of 1888 on his return from Tangier. Not only did he love painting seascapes; but he probably found ready buyers for them among the merchant ship owners whose company vessels he painted with such dash and vigour on the tossing waves.

The following year, according to a few pencilled notes in the front of an old sketch book, Alfred stayed in Grassington, near Skipton, from April until September. Following once again in Turner's footsteps, he visited many local beauty spots and big houses to sketch and possibly paint, including The Old Hall, Grassington; Kilnsey Crag, Hebden, and the picturesque old village of Linton with its riverside mill. Alfred probably had a quick chat with the washerwomen labouring at the tap and water troughs washing clothes as he sketched them in the corner of Grassington Market Place in September 1889; his sketch shows a quiet Yorkshire village, its houses solid and respectable where nowadays the tramping feet of thousands of visitors wear the new cobble stones smooth, and each elegant bay window has become a shop front.

Gate at the Kasba, 1888

Although Alfred had abandoned his pen and ink in favour of pencil again, he still worked hard to achieve the same depth and wealth of detail which had made his penwork so extraordinarily fine both in Tangier and on the Thames two years previously. In September he left Yorkshire for Corrie, on the Isle of Arran, where he spent autumn working in the vicinity of Loch Ranza and Glen Sannox before returning home to Bolton, where he based himself for the next eighteen months, trying to sell his work locally.

TIMBUCTOO MINSTRELS.

Morrocan Sketches

CAMELS IN THE SOKO

MOORISH "GHIMMELS"

A MOOR OF TANGIER

The house at Markland Hill with his younger brothers and sister all growing up together in it had little space for Alfred to paint; so he adopted the shed-in-the-garden tactic again, and built a small wooden cabin-type studio on land opposite his house, which was on the corner of the street. It would have provided him with peace and quiet and a little grey northern light to paint by, but few people wishing to purchase an original work of art would have stumbled on Alfred's studio in the mill district of Markland Hill. He took his work to Bromley's who both displayed and sold it, and during 1890 he travelled in the direction of the Lake District, stopping at Silverdale to paint.

There may be several reasons why Alfred chose to go to Norway in 1891. It was one of the most popular destinations for English travellers holidaying abroad at that time. They were made to feel very welcome by the Norwegians, most of whom spoke some English, and there were more English visitors to the fjords or tramping over the mountains than any other nationality. There was even an English church, St Olav's, built in Balestrand

CORNER OF MARKET PLACE
GRASSINGTON
SEP. 89.

Grassington Market Place, 1889

Bad News from the Cape, 1887

in 1897 to serve the English visitors, which is still open throughout the summer with a resident English vicar.

Or perhaps Alfred went to Norway entirely for art's sake. Maybe he studied the work of the Norwegian painters of the Munich and Düsseldorf German schools of painting, chief of whom was Hans Dahl; he, and several others in the 1850s, had popularised the genre of the village idyll, with his smiling fair-plaited maidens, set in sunny, smiling Nordic landscapes. Several artists of this genre returned to Norway and settled in the fjords, particularly Sognefjord, creating small communities of artists which have remained to this day. It was to Balestrand on Sognefjord that Dahl himself came to live, together with Augustin Normann. According to the Balestrand Tourist Guide:

"During the last century many artists found their way to Sogn to paint, several from the Art Academy of Düsseldorf. Some eventually settled in Balestrand and built villas, often using a romantic style with dragonhead ornamentation."

Alfred was just such an artist, with one exception. It wasn't from the elite academies of Düsseldorf or Munich that he made his way to Sogne, but from a garden shed in Bolton, where he packed his bags and headed for Balestrand by boat in July 1891.

Artists Villa, Balestrand

Thornton Force, Ingleton

Skjaeggedalfos, Hardanger Fjord, 1905

Chapter Three

Norway, a love affair

1889-1894

"To approach the Norwegian Coast at sunrise is an exceedingly enjoyable experience. Myriads of rock-islands in the sea and cloud-islands in the sky, their perspective terminating on the distant horizon in a peaked range of inland mountains, themselves like a cloud floating in golden vapour of dawn."

That particular description has a double significance. Not only is it the first paragraph of an English guide book to the Norwegian Fjords, but it also happens to be Alfred's own personal first impressions of the country he came to love so deeply. The book's title was *The Norwegian Fjords*, and its author was Alfred Heaton Cooper, painter, author and traveller.

Alfred can little have dreamt on that July day in 1891 when he approached the Norwegian Coast for the first time how great an influence this beautiful country and its hard-working people would have on him, and that one day he himself would be knowledgable enough about the geography of the fjords, and the customs of its people to write a popular guide book.

The book was written years later, and published in 1907 but the process of coming to know and love Norway so thoroughly began from the moment Alfred set foot on Norwegian soil, reached for his sketch book from the inside pocket of his jacket, and started to draw everything around him. He was very different from the archetypal Englishman abroad who spoke only his native tongue and expected everybody else to do so too. From the very first page of his sketch books, each subject he drew was given an English and a Norwegian name; thus the elegant little wooden carriole horse-drawn cart he travelled about in was also a *kariol*; two goats with horns locked in battle were *geiter* and a farm was a *gaard*. He appeared keen to learn the language, and must have relied on passers-by that he met to supply him with the Norwegian words he wanted to know.

First impressions are often lasting ones, and Alfred's experiences that summer certainly laid the foundations to a vast storehouse of general knowledge that he built up about the country. Collecting such a wealth of information would have been a gradual process; each subsequent visit to Norway added a little more.

Alfred's first journey follows the same route that his own book takes, up the Hardanger Fjord. In late July he was at Rosendal watching boat builders at work, and cruising by the Folgefonn glacier, which he saw from the deck of the *SS Hardangeren*. He was not only impressed by the grandeur of the scenery; his fascination was equally aroused by recording small articles of everyday life, such as the traditional curled loaf of bread, or *Norske Kringle*, and an old boathouse lock, to which the little rowing boats of Nordhejinsund were secured on the shore. On that same day, he met the demure *Helga* who posed for him in her simple blue dress and pinafore, and beside her, on the same page, lies a long wooden stick with sawn-off roots at one end, which Alfred enthusiastically catalogued as a *"porridge stirrer, made from a natural pine branch, about two feet long"*.

This relentless, if not pedantic determination to portray every aspect of Norwegian life, from boat locks to porridge stirrers, provided Alfred on later occasions with authentic detail both in his paintings and his writings. He had a natural curiosity but quite why he spent so much time that first summer collecting such minutiae is something of a mystery. Most English visitors and painters would, on a first visit, have been so overwhelmed with the majestic scenery of the fjords that drawing a pine porridge stirrer looking like a walking stick with curly roots might seem a little eccentric. But Alfred was far from the typical tourist.

Both the peasant children and the mountain goats gave Alfred good reason for pausing at the Bondhus glacier, Sundal, where he sketched the scenery and village life. His vigourous little drawings record what he saw with enthusiasm, and it is obvious that he was enjoying himself. It was in Sundal that he studied the first *kornloft* or *stabbur* that he had encountered. This farm outbuilding was roofed with turf, and Alfred himself defined it as a *"building which rests on short strong pillars of wood to keep out the rats and other intruders, and in it are stored dried meats, cheeses, milk and other foodstuffs"*.

Sundal itself had a church, a sprinkling of outlying farms and a jetty and steamer pier with the Norwegian flag flying, and Alfred took great pains to colour in his small sketch

Goddsund, Hardanger Fjord, 1891

Old boathouse lock

'Vikings!'

A 'saeter' near Odde, 1891

Porridge stirrer

Carriole

Sledge

with watercolours, perhaps as a guide to the colours he would use when he painted the scene again at some later date.

"Ullensvang," Alfred wrote, *"provides one of the most perfect fjord views to be had. This small place, in the Sor Fjord a few miles from Odda, has the reputation of being the fruit garden of Hardanger. It has been the favourite resort of artists and poets for generations. Here we see, across the narrow fjord, the huge snowfield and glacier of Folgefond stretching in undulating line along the graceful mountain masses. Near at hand stands the mediaeval church on a green promontory, and along the margin of the graceful sweep of bay brightly painted farms nestle in extensive orchards."*

With scenery like this, how could Alfred bear to let his eyes wander from undulating mountain masses, waterfalls, glaciers, sunsets and dawns? But while his fellow painters, perched precariously on rocky outcrops, toiled to capture such beauty, and the poets chewed their pencils in pursuit of words to convey such grandeur, Alfred was busy sketching down in the graveyard, or the mill, or the dairy.

He watched people at work, or living their ordinary, everyday lives. He watched women visiting loved ones in the cemetery, heads bowed in reverence beside the ancient nordic crosses. He observed washing day and recorded it all in detail, the water heated out of doors on little fires, the women bending over the tubs, scrubbing and squeezing, the steam rising in the sharp air, and a huge black cauldron left to heat on the fire while the washing was pegged out on a line slung between two trees. The landscape is majestic but its importance was only as background to the line of kerchiefs and nightshirts. Gathering firewood was a daily chore, and usually one that fell to the women. Alfred must have worked very swiftly to sketch one old lady walking towards him, weighed under with a massive load of kindling which was strapped to her back.

Life on the *saeter* or summer pasture land gave Alfred every possible opportunity to watch local families at work on their farms as he explored the Hardanger Fjord. There are several pages devoted to the customs of the *saeter* in Alfred's own guide book to Norway. It is unlikely that he ever made extensive notes as he learned about people and things. Instead, he sketched, drew and painted, making visual notes instead of written ones. This is his own description of a *saeter* or "mountain out-farm" which is probably taken directly from Alfred's numerous sketches:

"Many of the peasants who live alongside the fjords are also owners of large portions of the mountain plateaux in their neighbourhood, and on these excellent grazing is found in the summer months.

"When the heavy work of the spring has been finished on the home farm, and the snow has left these highlands, and when the vegetation has had time to establish itself anew, the whole farm household gets ready to remove the domestic animals to the saeter. It is a picturesque sight, this cavalcade, the animals all confusion, cattle lowing and sheep bleating, their bells tinkling

merrily as they skip about, the sturdy little ponies, heavily laden with necessary goods and chattels bringing up the rear. All seem full of glee that they can now have a few months of ideal grazing on those high lands after their imprisonment indoors all the long winter.

"Climbing and struggling onwards up the steep valley, then through almost trackless regions of rocks and stunted trees, they at length arrive at their destination, often after some fifteen or twenty miles of travelling.

"At the saeter they rest for the summer months amid rich vegetation by the margin of a lake or mountain tarn, surrounded by high mountain-tops. Here they graze on the bosky slopes to the music of babbling brooks.

"The saeter houses are mostly small and low, of one storey only; they are usually of a very primitive type, being, in fact, the earliest style of house building now in existence in the country, this ancient form surviving here long after it had been abandoned in the home farms. Attached to the dwelling house, or forming part of it, is a dairy where butter and cheese are made...

"... the women and girls only live up at the saeter, and in addition to the cheese and butter making, they must attend to their domestic animals during the four longest summer months.

"The men come up from the home farm at the week-ends with the necessary provisions, and take back with them the produce of the saeter.

"Bracing is the rarified air of these high lands; and although the sun's heat is great, it is tempered by the breezes which come from the snow-field or glacier on the higher mountains around."

Alfred Heaton Cooper - artist or anthropologist? Alfred's travels in Norway reveal that he was both, and could have made his career in either of these disciplines. Did he really acquire such education and command of English in some elementary school for mill families in a poor suburb of Bolton?

By September, 1891, Alfred had reached Oppedal, Ullensvang, just in time to watch the *saeter* workers sending bales of hay down the hillside attached to a running trip wire. This hay had been dried on the *saeter* by the simple expedient of cutting it and weaving sheafs of it round wooden poles stuck vertically in the ground. Everywhere he went, Alfred filled pages of notebooks with cows and sheep, goats and horses; each rough sketch is dated and the title written in both English and Norwegian.

Alfred was almost too busy sketching anything from a harness or horse collar to a strompe maes, or milk churn, to notice the spectacular scenery at Ullensvang, except as a background to peasant life. On September 12 he stopped at a popular beauty-spot looking towards Folgefond and sketched the fjord and mountains. There was the fjord, sparkling far below; waterfalls, ravines, and rocks could have tumbled willy-nilly all over his sketchbook. Instead it was *Herr Haffner - Sketching* which really caught Alfred's attention, seated above him, be-hatted and completely pre-occupied in his work oblivious of the role he was playing in a small artistic joke.

Helga

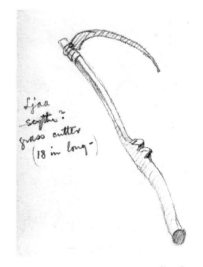

Scythe

Norske Kringle

Farm implements were examined and sketched and occasionally their particular use explained in brief notes. From these, we learn that the scythe was called a ljaa and measured 18 inches, while its bigger version had a five foot long shaft with a two foot blade. A simple device, called a *draa* and used for dragging down leaves and branches from the mountain for winter fodder also earned itself a place in the sketchbook; drawn like an original design on one page, Alfred next sketched the sledge-like *draa* in action, harnessed to a horse and transporting a massive load of firewood down from the mountain to provide winter fuel.

Throughout September, he looked at people working in the vicinity of Ullensvang, and recorded the results in his sketch books. There were potato pickers and fishermen, haymakers and dryers, wood gatherers, washer women, grass cutters and milkmaids, and a blacksmith.

left: Girl sweeping

below: Romsdal Fjord from Noes

On October 10th, he met Johannes Eidnes, a fisherman whose creased old face smiled with friendliness as Alfred sketched him. With the brim of his sou'wester turned up, his beard and whiskers made him look like the salty old skipper he probably was. If this face was instantly recognisable to generations of sardine eaters as the face featured on advertisements for Skippers sardines, then it may be no coincidence. Among Alfred's greatest admirers was the wealthy food manufacturer who produced the then famous Skippers brand. He was particularly fond of Alfred's Norwegian paintings, and bought them from Newcastle. It isn't beyond the bounds of possibility that the face of Johannes Eidnes, as drawn by Alfred, helped tinned sardines to become part of the British way of life.

Herr Haffner sketching, 1891

Alfred finally arrived on the Sognefjord at the beginning of November, after four months *en route* via Hardanger. One of the first little things that caught his eye was a *scaut*, a bonnet edged with pie-frills worn by married ladies which he immediately noted down in his sketch book.

Did he reach Balestrand on November 16th intending to stay there? Was this picturesque little village with its two resident artists, Normann and Dahl, really Alfred's proposed journey's end? Perhaps he did, for his new sketchbook starts with a bold announcement on the inside cover:

"A. Heaton Cooper (Landscapsmaler), Balholmen, Sogn, Norway, 1891... (from Bolton, England)".

Skippers Sardines can label

Such an address has a permanency about it, more than one would expect of the passing traveller. Alfred had arrived.

He at once sought out some of the artefacts of everyday peasant living which held such appeal for him. He sketched fishing boats and goat-houses, chickens and goats and even an ancient door handle. With the days getting shorter, he used the long hours of lamplight to read Viking history and literature, and one of his first Sogn drawings took him to the Cairn of King Bale, Balestrand, Sogn, which is marked with a crown and ancient initials underneath, and Alfred's own reference: *"See Tegner's 'Frithjof's Saga'"*. He never forgot the powerful Saga, and nearly ten years later, he named his second son after the Saga's hero, Frithjof.

Fascinated by the magical imagery of Norse legends, he even copied a panel painted on board the *SS Fjaler* depicting a curious leprachaun-like creature lighting a clay pipe and wearing a 'Noddy' hat with a bell on the end. Alfred was becoming so fluent in Norwegian, he no longer bothered to translate his sketch titles into English. Not that *"Norske Bergtrol!!"* needed translation. Mis-shapen trees bent into wild shapes with ghoulish faces lean over to frighten a poor young maiden running through the wood; Alfred's cartoon is poking gentle fun at the Gothic-horror of troll terror. One can almost hear him chuckle as he marked the title with not just one, but two exclamation marks.

Panel on board SS Fjaler

Norske Bergtrol!!

To learn so much about Norwegian life, language and culture in such a short time and to be, so rapidly, in sympathy with its customs and way of life could never have been achieved without the co-operation of the people Alfred met. He was travelling alone, a tall foreigner who sat patiently watching the peasants doing the washing, or milking the cows or cutting the hay - and then stood at his easel and drew or painted such activities, while other artists perched on crags looking at mountains and sunsets. The curiosity he aroused must have initiated many a conversation with the farmers and peasants. No doubt he would point to an object, an old lock or broom or bucket or whatever he was sketching, and when the corresponding word in Norwegian had been supplied, he would write it down carefully, delighted to be adding another word to his growing vocabulary.

Alfred seem to have preferred the company of local people to that of his fellow artists - a perfect way in which to learn Norwegian and become immersed in its country ways. Throughout his life, those who knew him spoke most generously of his friendly nature and popularity, and from the time Alfred arrived at Balholm in November, 1891, he attracted the kindly attentions of the village folk, although the sight of yet another visiting artist in an area so popular among painters cannot have been uncommon. Perhaps it was his consuming interest in their lives, the endearing way he tried out his newly-learnt Norwegian on them, and the fascination he had for drawing the people themselves and their simple habits which made him a little different from the usual run of English tourists and European painters.

He found himself a room in a bed and breakfast establishment run by the Kvikne family, not far from the *Fargarstova*, or dyer's house. Rasmus Valentinsen was a wool dyer who settled in Balholm in the 1870s, and had become known as the best dyer in the west of Norway. He made his own organic dyes from mosses, bark, seaweed and other plants, and each spring the farmers from outlying villages would come over on skis carrying big bundles of material on their backs which their wives had woven during the long winter nights. The farmers would be put up in barns all around Balholm during their stay while the dyeing was done. Rasmus Valentinsen won his reputation because of the subtlety of his shades and colours. The farmers' wives themselves sometimes made their own dye - but anyone who was at all particular about dyeing and colours went to Mr Valentinsen.

Rasmus Valentinsen had a large family; eight children by a first marriage, four of whom had died along with their mother, and a further six children when he re-married. The family lived in the tiny Dyer's Cottage, which was also Rasmus's workshop.

Alfred's first encounter with the Valentinsen family may well have been to see the dyer at work; he had certainly met them within a month or so of arriving at Kvikne's house, and knew one of the daughters, Mathilde, well enough to be invited to sign her autograph book at Christmas time. His

The Hunter's Return on Long Ski

At Balholm, 1891

Rasmus Valentinsen

The Dyer's Wife

message, carefully written in capital letters, and in English, is affectionate, yet rather formal. If he already looked at the bonny Mathilde with her dark hair and rosy cheeks with anything other than good wishes for her future, his words betray nothing of his feelings, as he wrote this message to the girl who would eventually become his wife and companion for life:

To Mathilde, With the best of Good Wishes for your future welfare - yes, and may your life be a long and happy one - and may I never forget Balholmen and yourself. AHC.

The message is written in the top right-hand corner of the page, the rest of which is devoted to a delicate little watercolour of Balholm in winter, the trees bare, the mountains snow-covered and a horse-drawn sledge gliding along the snowy track which ran by the fjord.

The autograph book has few other entries, all in Norwegian except for a rather mysterious contribution dated 1893, written in English. It is a rather pious and sentimental little poem entitled *"Sunday School Work"* which encourages the cultivation of virtue, growth and goodness like a flower in the human soul. The poem was signed simply *"WC"*. Perhaps Matilde deliberately collected the autographs of visiting poets and painters.

The book lay forgotten among Alfred's sketch books for many years after his death and it was only idle curiosity which brought his first encounter with Mathilde to light again, one hundred years later. The cover of the little grey book has been decorated very delicately by an unknown hand. The word *Album* is inscribed across it, with the capital A forming part of a tree branch upon which a little bird sits, with yellow breast and bright little red head. There is a familiarity about the way in which the bird is painted,

TO MATHILDE, WITH THE BEST OF GOOD WISHES FOR YOUR FUTURE WELFARE — YES & MAY YOUR LIFE BE A LONG AND A HAPPY ONE — & MAY I NEVER FORGET BALHOLMEN & YOURSELF

A·H·C·

YULETIDE 1891

A page by Alfred in Mathilde Valentinsen's autograph book, 1891

a strong likeness to the hummingbird Alfred had done twelve years before in the style of John Ruskin. Perhaps Alfred's was the unknown hand which painted Mathilde's book cover.

Much of Norwegian country life was centred around the church, which provided an opportunity to meet the neighbours regularly, as well as being the place where the most important social events happened, be they weddings or funerals. In the months following that first Christmas in Balholm, Alfred's interest in the role of the church in community life led him to explore churches, worship and traditions, especially bridal customs.

Here is his description, from his own book, of Sunday worship:

"It is an interesting sight to witness on Sunday mornings the well-filled boats coming from all parts of the fjord parish, men and girls alike rowing their graceful boats to church. On landing, they arrange each other's toilet on the beach, and when inside the sacred edifice, the women and girls sit on one side of the centre aisle and the men on the other.

"The service is Lutheran, and there is much singing of hymns or 'psalmer' in a leisurely way while sitting. The farmer's dog is also a 'regular attender' but he is usually well-behaved, and no one appears to take the slightest notice of him unless he happens to pick a quarrel with another of his species.

"After, and sometimes during Divine service, small groups of farmers may be seen in the churchyard talking over the state of the market - or crops and cattle and other gossip - each one repeatedly turns over the ample 'quid' of tobacco in his mouth. It may be that they meet only one in two or three weeks, for many a parson has two or three churches to attend to. But the churches are, as a rule, well-filled, no matter what happens to be the condition of the weather."

The churches themselves, particularly the wooden stav structures dating back to pagan times were of great interest to Alfred, being the finest example of ancient traditional wood carving still in existence in Norway. Towards the end of the last century, Norway had enjoyed a revival in traditional wood carving, and Alfred, who would have been well-versed in pre-Raphaelite craftsmanship, appreciated the carver's skills at first hand:

"...cleverly designed and skilfully executed work in wood - dragons and other grotesque motifs from pagan mythology being worked into exquisite pattern on high-backed chair, massive sideboard and roomy settle."

But the ancient carving of the stav churches, according to Alfred, still represented the best in Norwegian carving:

"Wood carving in Norway is one of the most ancient of the industrial arts, and it shows a well-connected development from the days of the Vikings, who carved in bold design the figure-heads which ornamented their warships. But the most interesting and important period of this art is seen in the massive and richly-carved doorways to the wooden stav churches.

"The earliest of these show distinct evidence of Irish influence, the ornament being usually composed of ribbon festoon, with grotesque figures of animals and snakes. The most characteristic of these carvings date from the eleventh and twelfth centuries."

The ancient door of Vik Church, Sogn, impressed Alfred so greatly early in 1892 that it earned itself a few brief hand-written notes in addition to the usual sketch:

"...Chinese looking figures painted on woodwork; much old carving round doorway and inside church. The church some 650 years old, the inside adorned with idols somewhat resembling Buddhist."

This fascination for church architecture extended to the ceremonies which took place within the ancient buildings, particularly marriage.

Brides and weddings seemed to be at the forefront of Alfred's mind during the spring of 1892, perhaps because he already had his sights set on Mathilde and dreamt of the day when his own wedding would take place among the fjords. The first wedding he attended was on February 11, 1892, at Tjugum Church, where he sketched the bride and groom kneeling together at the circular altar rail in front of the minister. Just a few days later, Alfred painted a *"Brud - Balholm"*, who posed for him wearing her traditional bridal crown festooned with coloured ribbons which flowed down the back.

Vik Church, Sogn

Alfred's meticulous research even led him to the place where the bride's trousseau was stored:

"An additional outbuilding, called a bui is used for keeping the clothing, tapestries, blankets etc. also the daughter's wedding trousseau and old silver articles - heirlooms - including a bride's crown of silver gilt, all stored away in huge chests ('kists'). Here may also be found carefully treasured a variety of ancient carved and painted wooden bowls and tankards, out of use except at weddings and other state occasions."

The next wedding he attended was on March 1st, again at Tjugum when the groom was Johannes Ese of Balholm. Perhaps this family and other families too had commissioned Alfred to paint the happy couples at spring weddings up and down the fjord because there was no local photographer's studio to record such important events.

This is what Alfred learnt about wedding customs as he visited churches and nuptials, and eventually married in Balholm himself:

"Another old custom still survives in this district of Sogn. When it becomes known that two young people are to be engaged to be married, the boys in the district shoot into the air with rifles, and fire small cannon around the house on the evening when the young man goes to ask of the parents their consent to the engagement. They also ring hand-bells and blow a horn; these noises must surely prove rather disconcerting to the newly betrothed.

"In some cases the prospective bridegroom has many miles of rowing along the fjord before he reaches the home of his lady-love. His visit is usually paid at the end of the week, and he generally spends the night there. As a practical joke, the peasant boys have been known to take his boat, drag it up on shore, and hide it in some secluded place, much to his great discomfort and annoyance when he wishes to return in the morning.

"At all large weddings, to which may be invited from 150 to 200 guests, festivities are usually kept up for a week or more.

"Dancing and fiddling go on day and night continuously... the music to these dances is exceedingly lively, even barbaric in character, and the dances are consequently wild and exciting.

"Each wedding party engage their own fiddler, and he it is who leads the procession from the farm to the church door, and it often occurs that several weddings take place at the same church at the same time."

Wedding of Johannes Ese, 1892

Springtime was a favourite season for weddings, before the women left their husbands to start the serious farm work of summer up at the saeter. Taking advantage of the better weather and lengthening daylight, Alfred's sketchbooks show how far he travelled around and about to capture the beauty of the Sognefjord region. Many of his drawings were done from a rowing boat on the water looking towards the shore; but on other occasions, he spent a night or two away from Balholm when the peasant hospitality was such that Alfred felt compelled to recall it later in his own book. This is a trip that he made to Naero Fjord, Sogn, retold years later:

"At a lonely farm, situated in the wildest part of the Næroy Fjord, it was my happy fortune to stay for some days in the merry month of May. On my arrival there, and in compliance with a signal from the shore, the steamer slows up and a boat is brought alongside. A friendly goodbye to the obliging captain and I am rowed ashore where I meet the kind owner of the farm, my host. He and his good wife (kone) show me through the house, an excellent example of a 'bonders' home of the olden time.

"The principal living-room is about twenty feet square. The walls display unusually thick baulks of timber, while the huge beams show distinctly the marks of the axe which fashioned them. The heavy doors are nearly square in shape, with lock and handle of antique design in wrought iron. On one side of this room stands an elevated open hearth (peis), over which hangs a crane, and to this is attached a huge copper cauldron. The smoke from the peat fire escapes through the roof from a very wide chimney. A clean-scrubbed massive table almost fills one end of the room by the side of the wall benches. High-backed chairs, several spinning wheels and a carpet weaving frame help to fill up this spacious apartment.

"To reach the room set apart for me I must climb up wooden ladder-like steps. My room, simply but comfortably furnished, was fresh and clean. On the left side, in a dark corner, was the customary low, wooden, box-like bed, which I saw at a glance was, for one of my stature, much too short. It was piled high with some soft material on the top, This covering proved on examination to be a 4-feet square air-tight bag containing eiderdown about a foot deep. Under this was only the thinnest cotton sheet and I began to wonder how these two as a covering could possibly remain together in harmony throughout the night, and as to whether they were calculated to cover all one's limbs at one and the same time.

"On being very considerately asked on the following morning how I had slept, and if I would like an extra eiderdown on, I courteously but firmly declined.

"At 8am. came breakfast-time. On the table were placed several kinds of native cheese, brown bread, butter and potato cakes, dried mutton and boiled potatoes, four boiled eggs and a large bowl of creamy milk. In addition to these delicacies, a cup of excellent coffee was brought in. The meal nearly ended, and not having made much impression on this mass before me, the good wife again invited me - almost co-erced me - 'to make a good meal' and seemed quite disappointed that my capacity was so limited.

"Similar fare was my portion for the other meals, varied only with boiled goat's flesh, ptarmigan, and hare or wild reindeer.

"These kind-hearted people did all in their power to make my stay comfortable. They enjoyed a little gossip from the world outside their fjord, and it was interesting to hear them talk in their very pronounced and ancient dialect (Sognemaal) which is as unlike modern Norwegian 'as she is spoke' as the English of Chaucer's time is to our own modern tongue."

Back at Balestrand, Alfred watched the way in which the women of the family worked on their own home-grown wool, and he sketched each stage of the carding, spinning, winding and weaving and even carpet-making which took place in the living room of many homes, using an ancient wheel and a wooden hand-loom. Coming as he did from a Lancashire mill town, this primitive cottage industry must have been of particular interest to Alfred, whose own mother had made his career as an artist possible by the many hours she spent weaving at the loom.

By the spring of 1892, Alfred realised that he would have to leave all the newly-discovered pleasures of Norway and head for home. Sooner or later, he would have been obliged to sell some of his paintings in Balholm just to pay his living expenses at Kvikne's. Perhaps he had been living off the money he had received from commissions at home the year before; but with Hans Dahl and Augustine Normann as the competition, he had very little chance of selling his Balholm landscapes to discerning visitors. Many of them, searching for a suitable keepsake of the fjords, would be loth to buy a landscape from a young Englishman only recently arrived in the area when two of the better-known Norwegian exponents of the genre actually lived and painted in Balholm.

Jostedal Glacier, Fjaerland Fjord

But Alfred himself had noticed the growing popularity of Norwegian holidays with the English, who found the North Sea crossing quick and convenient to reach such a beautiful destination. Many of them who had spent challenging days on the glaciers or hiking in the mountains might like something hanging on the wall to remind them of such beautiful Nordic scenery, but without the inconvenience of transporting a picture home by *karriol*, coach, boat and train; and perhaps such a picture by the young, unknown Alfred might appeal more to the English pocket?

So when, in June 1892, Alfred left Mathilde Valentinsen in Balholm and headed, regretfully, for Bergen and the boat home, he travelled via Newcastle, and took the trouble to stop en route at Swan & Morgan, well-known Newcastle art dealers. With premises near the boat terminal, it was just the sort of gallery that travellers to and from Norway might visit to while away the odd hour. His hunch proved correct; his work proved popular with North Sea crossing passengers and Swan & Morgan handled dozens of his paintings over many years.

Leaving Mathilde must have been difficult for Alfred. He promised to write - it would have to be in Norwegian; but what chance would his halting and hesitant prose have against the rival attentions of the strong, handsome Viking men who inhabited the fjords, and who saw Mathilde daily? Sensibly, Alfred wasted no further time, and on his return he did indeed write to Mathilde - to propose marriage. He told her it would take him a year or so to save enough money for them to get married, and asked Mathilde if she would wait for him.

Her reply was swift. She told Alfred that she truly loved him, and that she would wait for him until they could be wed. She was true to her word.

Alfred had returned to the studio and family home at Markland Hill and spent the next two years experimenting with subject matter, not always very successfully. There were the usual trips to Scotland and the Lake District to paint landscapes, which sold quite well through his Bolton art dealers, Bromley's of 32 Bradshawgate. Occasionally the surprised residents of Markland Hill were treated to an art exhibition within their midst when Alfred's initiative would transform his little shed temporarily into a gallery, to see what he could sell himself directly to the public.

The countryside was not the only landscape subject Alfred wanted to paint. Living in Bolton, he was as familiar with industrial landscape as with the moorland he had first painted as a fourteen-year-old. On October 31, 1892, Alfred sat in a cornfield by the Leeds & Liverpool Canal at Wigan looking across the murky water at the coal, iron and steel works opposite. The picture he composed and planned across four pages of his sketchbook was entitled *Coal and Iron Versus Corn - Wigan*, and it was to be his entry to the next Royal Academy exhibition. Dozens of chimneys sent billows of smoke and steam into the atmosphere, the furnaces were to glow yellow and red, and pigeons and rooks picked over the sheafs of "grimy, smokey-

Coal and Iron versus Corn - Wigan, 1892

looking corn" which were heaped in the foreground, defiantly standing their ground in the face of ugliness and industrial waste. An airshaft from the mine beneath surfaced within the poor-looking field, and the Rosebridge pits and St. Catherine's Church, Ince, were to form the farthest boundary of this horizontal study which, Alfred noted on his page, would measure 6ft by 4ft.

The culture shock Alfred must have suffered by leaving his Norwegian idyll to return home to an area which had suffered the very worst excesses of the industrial revolution perhaps inspired him to paint such grim little moral tales as *Coal and Iron Versus Corn - Wigan*. Needless to say, his reflective sortie into environmental realism was less impressive to the selection committee at the Royal Academy than his previous successful entry of a picturesque Scottish landscape. *Coal and Iron Versus Corn - Wigan* subsequently failed to appear at the exhibition. The following year he returned to a more conventional style and *A Woodland Path - Autumn* reinstated him with the Royal Academy.

Turning the pages of his sketchbook in autumn of 1892, one is suddenly transported back to Norway and Mathilde by the frequent small impressions of Norwegian women wearing traditional costume, or dancing, or skating. Uncharacteristically, these sketches are not dated; this must have been because they were drawn from memory, and lack some of the sharper detail

Lancashire cornfield

Deane Church, 1892

of previous work, being affectionate, quick little thoughts which Alfred put down on paper to satisfy his longing.

In December 1892, Alfred stood his easel in the snow just a mile or so from his home in Bolton and painted Deane Church, a most ancient and attractive parish church which has been an important centre of worship over a widespread area for nearly five hundred years and probably longer. The epitaphs on the oldest graves date back to the late 1600s, and the snowscape which Alfred painted most competently still hangs within Deane Church.

That same month, Alfred was admitted to the third degree of Freemasonry, and became a full member of the Horwich Lodge the following February.

A series of painted sketches labelled *Decoration of Deane Church* indicate that Alfred was experimenting with the design of stained glass windows. There is some evidence to suggest that he may have been competing for a commission to design windows for the church. The sketch books reveal considerable research into the English martyrs, with a journey to Cambridge to copy portraits of Nicholas Ridley, from Pembroke College Hall and Ridley Hall Chapel; and of Martin Luther from the Fitzwilliam Museum. But the backwaters of Cambridge proved irresistable to Alfred, who left the venerable martyrs to go for a walk around the town to sample the real delights of such a famous place. He found them, for there, sure enough, buried among the giants of martyrdom in his sketch book is *Goode's Boat Sheds, Cambridge*, which doubtless brought back happy memories of Alfred's own boating days as a student, rowing up the Thames to Shillingford.

Goode's Boat Sheds
Cambridge, 1894

"Beda", 1894

Alfred also went to Lambeth Palace to copy a portrait of Matthew Parker, Archbishop of Canterbury, and the completed sketches include Cranmer, Latimer and Ridley, Venerable Bede, St Columba, John Wyclif, Matthew Parker and the Deane martyr himself, George Marshe, pictured by Alfred in pious prayer, with Deane Church providing a suitably recognisable landscape behind.

This sort of commission was outside Alfred's previous experience but he was no doubt in need of income from whatever sources he could find. For an artist who liked nothing better than to paint outdoors, he must have been frustrated by the constraints on his originality that this work imposed

The Martyrs' windows are there, certainly; and Deane Church is proud enough of them to include their origins and history in a short guide to the Church's coloured glass windows. The George Marshe window was erected by Mr James Boardman, a long-serving church warden at Deane, in thankfulness of his forty years of marriage. The artist and designer are not mentioned; but just a glimpse at the three lights of the window reveal that they were based on biblical interpretations of Faith, Hope and Charity, and bear no resemblance whatsoever to Alfred's finished designs, or the English martyrs.

In spite of the lengths to which he went in his interpretation of the martyrdom theme, researching, copying, designing and painting, his designs were never used and the commission was obviously awarded to someone else. There are no Heaton Cooper windows in Deane Church or anywhere else.

Turned down by the Royal Academy, rejected by his local parish church and hundreds of miles away from the place and person he longed for most, Alfred must have felt depressed. Nothing other than a morbid depression could have inspired him, on March 19th 1894, to draw the macabre and ghoulish sketch which he entitled *There is a Reaper whose Name is Death*. Alfred's grim reaper is the usual skeleton, gaping mouth stretched back in death, whose bones are draped in the gentle folds of a loose gown. The skeleton holds one hand out, as though in warning, and slung over the other shoulder is an enormous scythe. Perhaps this powerful reminder of man's mortality was copied from an earlier age, when death stalked the plague-stricken streets of Europe - or perhaps it was a product of Alfred's temporary frustration, or an undercurrent of grief and rage which dated back to his mother's early death. The drawing looks all the more out of character, surrounded as it is in his sketch books with soft images of ladies reading in the park and leafy landscapes. It is quite out of keeping with his easy temperament and genial nature and the only attempt at depicting the macabre he is known to have made.

After three years of waiting, working and saving, Alfred was in a position to write to Mathilde to arrange a date for their marriage, in the autumn of 1894.

In order to comply with Norwegian regulations, Alfred obtained a copy of his birth certificate in August 1894. In the same month in preparation for his forthcoming marriage, he was required by the Norwegian church to make a written statement in the presence of a witness. The statement reads as follows:

"In accordance with Norwegian church regulations respecting foreign marriages, I hereby make the following solemn declaration:

1. That I, Alfred Heaton Cooper.

2. Residing at Markland Hill, Heaton, Bolton, England, am by profession an artist (painter of pictures).

3. I was born at Regent Terrace, Halliwell, Bolton, England on the 14th day of June 1863.

4. That my father's name is William Cooper - who is a cashier at Cotton Mills in Bolton, England.

5. That I have not been married before.

6. That I was vaccinated in 1863 and not since, but have been in the enjoyment of good health all my life.

7. That I belong to the Church of England (Protestant) having been baptised and confirmed into that Church.

8. That I am not bound by any other marriage promise.

As witness my hand this twenty-seventh day of August

Eighteen hundred and ninety-four

Signed - Alfred Heaton Cooper"

"There is a Reaper whose name is death", 1894

Witness to the signature:

"I hereby certify that all the above statements respecting Mr A. Heaton Cooper are correct and I can testify from personal knowledge for the period since 1877, when I became Vicar of the Ancient Parish of Deane.

Signed and witnessed by me

H. Sheridan Patterson

Vicar of Deane and Surrogate for Marriage Licences

Dated this 27th Augt 1894"

Armed with this solemn declaration and his birth certificate, Alfred packed his brushes, paintbox, easel and best suit and set off for Balholm in September to marry Mathilde Marie Valentinsen.

Fanden, Alfred's dog,

Flag Day, Lord Street, Southport, 1896

Chapter Four

Hard Times

1894-1906

"Mathilde was very bonny. She had dark hair and bright eyes, really wide-open eyes and when she was young she must have been a very attractive young person. I'm not at all surprised at my father falling for her, but they really loved each other; after all, they waited for three years while he saved enough to get married. That showed that one person was enough for her, there was only one person and that was Alfred."

The love that Mathilde and Alfred shared, one for the other, was obvious to all who knew them throughout their married life, especially their children; and it was their younger son, William, who used those words to describe his parents' relationship.

They were both the same age - thirty-one years at the time of their marriage, which took place in a church already familiar to Alfred, where he had attended several weddings in the spring of 1892. Mathilde had been brought up in the Norwegian Lutheran Church, but despite her belief in God, she also had a simple country faith in the existence of earth spirits which figure so vividly in Norse folklore.

To reach Tjugum Church, the bride and groom and their guests had to row across Ese Fjord, dressed in their traditional Norse costume. The ancient wood-built church was very light inside, with clear glass windows looking out over the fjord to the mountains beyond. This is how Alfred described a typical fjord wedding in his guide book - his own wedding must have been very similar:

"The wedding bryllups was to be celebrated that morning, and everybody was now ready except the bride, whose friends were engaged in adding the final touches to her maidenly toilet. A start is soon made, first a kind of informal procession along the short stretch of road to the pier, and a

Towards Tjugum Church, 1892

scramble into the boats, then out on the fjord, their oars keeping time to the strains of the fiddle. They row along pleasantly for a couple of miles, and then arrive at the small wooden church..."

"...The wedding service over, the whole party, the clergyman now included, return to the inn to partake of the wedding feast and to drink the healths of the bride and groom. The festivities are prolonged with hearty excitement, eating, drinking, and dancing the Halling-fling and Spring dance day and night for over a week."

Such celebrations were not always peaceful affairs, especially when more than one wedding took place at once, which was quite a common practice. It was essential to engage the very best fiddler available to lead the procession to the church door, and there was fierce competition between rival fiddlers. But this competitiveness extended to the dancing as well:

"This same spirit of rivalry also possesses the younger men; each vies with the others in the skill and cleverness in the dances, in which their ability to kick the highest is put to the test for the admiration and applause of the onlooking girls. This rivalry would result at times in quite a battle royal of words and, even more seriously, it would end in real danger to life and limb."

Alfred and Mathilde's marriage, being an autumn wedding, would have escaped the frantic fiddling and dangerous dancing that spring weddings inspired. It would have been an altogether quieter affair, especially as Alfred had no family or supporters there to swell the numbers and add to the general gaiety. But for all that, the romance of rowing to church, accompanied by a fiddler, followed by the celebrations of the *bryllup* were a far cry from the muted proceedings that might have taken place if Alfred and Mathilde had been married in the quiet solemnity of Deane Church, or St Peter's, Halliwell.

One can easily imagine the dullness of an English Victorian wedding by comparison; Alfred and Mathilde walking quietly to church through the dank grey mist of an autumn morning in Bolton, the trees dripping on irregular rows of old graves, the path slippery with rotting leaves and inside the church the hesitant old clergyman waiting to marry the couple, with the pew opener and verger looking on. What good fortune for Alfred and Mathilde that instead of a Bolton wedding, they began married life with all the fun and jollity that made every fjord wedding a memorable event, and spent their honeymoon afterwards in such beautiful, tranquil surroundings.

And if the villagers of Halliwell had let off rockets and lined the streets to provide an enthusiastic send off for the happy couple, it would have been a matter for an officer of the law... but this is what the people of Balholm did when Mr Alfred and Mrs Mathilde Heaton Cooper left the village to make their home back in England. Mathilde brought with her a young girl from Balholm as a companion and maid, and the three of them left Norway on November 4th.

Balholm in Autumn

It was Guy Fawkes night as they docked in Newcastle on the evening of November 5th. Seeing the rockets, fireworks and bonfires, Mathilde in all innocence remarked to Alfred: *"Isn't it kind of the English to give us such a grand welcome!"*

But the welcome was short-lived, as Mathilde was to find out in their first few months living at Blue Bonnet Hall, in a suburb of Bolton called Over Hulton. Foreigners living or even visiting Bolton in the 1890s were extreme rarities. Neither Mathilde nor her companion spoke English; and the sight of Mathilde with the young girl, who dressed in her Norwegian peasant costume, was soon the object of much vulgar curiosity, especially in the shops where the two women, with no English, could only point at things to indicate what they wanted to buy. Mathilde's sense of isolation must have increased dramatically when the young maid could stand it no longer and returned to Norway.

By this time, Mathilde was pregnant, and the couple's first child, Sverre, was born in 1895 in Bolton. With no mother or even mother-in-law to help the 33-year-old Mathilde with her first confinement, and no sisters living nearby to advise on babycare and feeding, Mathilde must have felt extremely lonely, especially as Sverre was not a strong baby and did not thrive in the smokey, polluted air of industrial Bolton.

Sverre was fair-haired, with blue eyes and a placid expression in a patient, resigned little face. Alfred sketched his son peacefully sleeping in his crib, rocked by Mathilde as she snatched a moment to herself, a book propped against the cot. Sadly, despite a move to Southport in the hope that a little bracing sea air would help mother and child, Sverre never grew any stronger and he died of pneumonia at less than a year old.

Family history had repeated itself; Alfred and Mathilde had suffered the same cruel loss that Alfred's own parents had experienced. Baby Sverre died just as Rachel, Alfred's older sister, had died in infancy over thirty years before. Alfred and Mathilde's love only grew in strength as they comforted each other in their sadness. Had their marriage been anything less than a love match, Mathilde might well have packed her bags and gone home to Balholm forever. Maybe Alfred promised her then that one day, when his paintings had made him rich and famous, they would return to live in Norway.

The only memory of baby Sverre that Alfred and Mathilde kept was a portrait of him painted at about six months, dressed in a light blue colour which matched his weary little eyes.

Alfred had great hopes that life at 21, Morven Grove, Southport, and latterly 10, Nevill Street, Southport, would bring a change in his fortunes. He hoped that the wealthy and successful entrepreneurs of Manchester and Liverpool who had made Southport a fashionable watering place would patronise the arts by buying his paintings.

Putting landscape temporarily to one side, Alfred spent many hours out and about along the beach, the Promenade and the quiet lanes around Southport. His rough sketches are delightful little studies in contemporary fashions and mores; the fine weather in June 1896, encouraged ladies to sit and chat in the shade of parasols and under trees. In one drawing, a mother

Lord and Master

Sverre at six months

William Cooper, 1895

and her daughter share a book together on a park bench, while the gentleman next to them sleeps in contented oblivion, head back and mouth open. Another shows Lord Street to have been a very busy thoroughfare on June 25th, 1896. A policeman standing by the drinking fountain observes the hustle and bustle of the passers-by while two ladies take the weight off their feet, shopping baskets on their knees, deep in gossip, much to the annoyance of a young charge sitting to one side, her hands neatly folded, and an expression of blank boredom on her face.

There were boat races at Marine Lake on July 6th to celebrate Lifeboat Demonstration Day in Southport. A stall decorated with Chinese lanterns proclaimed: "Ball's Confetti Sold Here" and the day had a carnival atmosphere about it in Alfred's drawings. But was there really nude bathing for ladies on Southport beach as one of Alfred's sketches might suggest? If it wasn't mere fantasy, how did Alfred get a peep at the bare bottoms and voluminous knickerbockers displayed in this seaside frolic?

He walked the byways that summer, and during 1897 too, sketching picturesque thatched cottages, making notes about when they would look their best to paint. He doubtless hoped to sell such paintings to their occupants. Perhaps he knocked on cottage doors in the hope of a commission or sale. Mathilde, although interested in Alfred's work, never attempted to take up art herself. Hidden away in Alfred's Southport sketch book is the only example of anything she ever drew or painted. Sitting idly by while Alfred worked, perhaps he teased her into sketching the farmhouse he was drawing. The result, signed M. C., is labelled *'Storskjout... ha-ha'*. Mathilde was right about her absence of skill. The childish drawing was, indeed, a joke.

Alfred continued portrait painting, too. The lady *"C . . ."* dressed in blue silk who posed for Alfred in 1897, looking reflectively through the dainty veil of her black and peach coloured hat never actually bought the finished watercolour, because it remained among his unsold work. But perhaps he painted this attractive woman on impulse, on a whim of his own, so that he could enjoy the sight of her always without revealing her identity and causing scandal. She remains, her serenity as fresh as the day Alfred captured it, a fine example of Alfred's skill and ability in whatever field he chose to work.

Perhaps Alfred had more luck with the portrait of a young man, pictured playing with his dog beside a substantial looking house in the late Victorian mock-Gothic style. The sketch, bold and confident, has no title but *"Lord and Master"* would have been appropriate. The dog, a labrador, stands on its hind legs, front paws resting on his master's waistcoat as he tries to reach a titbit held temptingly above his nose - rather different from Alfred`s usual canine sitter, the family pet, a mongrel called Fanden who lived at Markland Hill and loved to chase the flies that tickled his nose, according to several affectionate and humourous little sketches dotted about amongst more serious subjects.

A Lady "C . . ."

The notes that Alfred made about the finished size of a picture usually indicated that it was an important work which he always completed, such as an exhibit for the Royal Academy. The importance of this particular dog picture, displaying wealth, control, power and position is that somebody was almost certainly paying Alfred to paint it.

Following baby Sverre's death in 1896, Mathilde became pregnant again that summer, and a little daughter, Alice Ellide Beate, was born in March, 1897. An affectionate little sketch of Ellide, made when she was eight months, shows an alert, chubby but rather serious baby. Fortunately, her health was more robust than Sverre's had been and the Southport air was better for her lungs than Bolton's fetid atmosphere had been for Sverre.

But Alfred and his family needed more than air to live on. Southport had fallen far short of Alfred's expectations. He had thought that the sort of wealthy people who lived and stayed at the resort would spend their newly earned money on buying class and culture, in the form of original art. He was dismayed and very disappointed to discover that the *nouveau riche* of Southport, recently arrived from amassing fortunes in the mills and factories of Liverpool and Manchester, knew little about art and cared even less about it. They were philistines, and materialism reigned supreme in fashionable Southport.

His work unsold and his family short of food, Alfred had no choice but to leave Southport. The doctor had warned him after Sverre died of pneumonia that Mathilde might follow suit, weakened as she was by frequent bronchial infections, unless she could live in a mountain climate similar to her native Norway. A move to the Lake District seemed to be the answer to several problems.

Hawkshead (moonlight)
12 November 1898

Windermere, Lakeside and Boats, 1890's

The air would be pure, the water clean; the mountains would glisten with snow in winter and shimmer dark purple in the long summer evenings, casting shadows across the tarns and lakes below. All this - and discerning, picture-buying visitors, too, Alfred must have thought. Unlike Southport, people of worth and education sought out the Lakes in pursuit of its resident poets and writers. But resident painters were not quite so thick on the ground as the elite circle of writers. Alfred decided to try his luck in the Lakes, and in 1898 he rented a tiny cottage in Hawkshead, just behind the Red Lion Hotel.

However cramped and primitive the little cottage was for the family to live in, Alfred wasted no time in taking immediate advantage of being within minutes or just a mile or two of whatever he wanted to draw and paint. The Lake District had provided him all his painting life with subject matter; only the previous year, the Royal Academy had selected his latest Lakeland painting, *Where the Ducks Dabble - Hawkshead* for the Summer Exhibition. Now, for the first time, it was fully accessible to him rather than half a day's expensive journey away. He was out and about, night and day; Hawkshead village by moonlight, painted from the cottage; Esthwaite Lake, one hazy evening in September; Graythwaite Old Hall, detail of the dovecote; Tent Lodge, Coniston... Newby Bridge... Sunny Bank, Torver... Yewdale Beck. He walked everywhere, carrying his easel and paints on his back. A bicycle might have been quicker, but difficult for transporting his gear.

Loading and carting timber, Holker Park, 1890

Living now as he did among the fells, Alfred might have been tempted to paint only landscapes, specifically for the growing number of visitors. But his Millet-inspired fascination for watching and then portraying ordinary people at work in their ordinary, everyday lives had not left him, and the traditional old Lakeland occupations provided Alfred with plenty of ideas. It was in September 1898 that he first began to watch the charcoal burners at work in the woodland and coppices around Hawkshead. Charcoal burning, as a woodland industry, was already starting to die out. There were cheaper ways of producing gun powder for the local quarries, and charcoal burning was primitive and labour intensive.

Alfred's drawings and paintings provide a comprehensive historical record of a dying skill; it was a subject he returned to several times in later years to observe the building of the charcoal pit, and the overnight "burn". Some charcoal burners brought their families to live in the woods during the summer months; a "burn" could not be left untended overnight because the smouldering fire had to be built up frequently and never allowed to flare up.

The woodmen and their loaded wagons of cut timber pulled by heavy horses was another source of fascination to Alfred, as were the char fishermen with their 'lathes' on Windermere and Coniston. Domestic life, too, seemed happier; Alfred sketched Mathilde standing by the fireside, with Ellide lying on the floor playfully tugging at her mother's skirts. *The Evening Meal* was painted about this time, another scene of happy domesticity. An elderly lady, perhaps Grandma, sits on a high-back wooden settle, baby on her knee, feeding it from a spoon. The plant on the window cill, the ready cradle nearby both give a homely feeling of simple contentment.

Flag Street, Hawkshead, 1902

Charcoal burners preparing the pit

*Interior of Charcoal burners' hut,
Bouth, 1908*

Church Hill, Hawkshead, 1902

*Hawkshead Old Hall
and Courthouse, 1902*

The following summer, Alfred and Mathilde returned to Norway for three months for the first time since their marriage five years before. While Mathilde enjoyed introducing Ellide to her grandparents and all her Norwegian family, Alfred sketched and painted tirelessly throughout the long summer days, concentrating this time on the variety of boats that travelled up and down the fjords; Ellide, his own daughter and eldest child, had been named after a Norwegian ship.

There were sailing yachts, and big steamers from Stavanger; rowing boats laden down with cut hay and others transformed into sailing boats, a birch

Mathilde and Ellide, by the fireside, 1897

Mathilde and Ellide, 1897

branch stuck in the bows acting as a sail. There was back-breaking potato picking on the farms to take Alfred's attention, and the standing corn was left bound to tall poles to dry, the grain facing south. But the sketches are rough and scanty in detail, almost frantic, perhaps because Alfred was spending more time on painting and less on preliminary sketches. It was, after all, a working holiday to help feed the family for the following year.

More visitors were coming to Balholm than ever before, and the Kvikne family's five room guest house where Alfred stayed on his first visit had been superceded by a sizeable hotel, built in the traditional manner in wood, with the reputation of being one of the finest hotels in the district. While staying in Balholm in that summer, Alfred made the acquaintance of a Russian prince from St Petersburg who was staying at the hotel. His name and address are scribbled by the side of a rough sketch, and the painting which Alfred completed at a later date was sent to Russia as a gift. It may have been a gesture of genuine friendship - but it could equally have been an attempt to impress the rich and famous which poor Alfred couldn't afford to miss. This was the letter of thanks his gift received, which Alfred thought worthy of keeping:

"Dear Sir,

Allow me to return you my sincere thanks for your kind attention in sending me the beautiful water colour, which afforded me great pleasure. I am really very grateful to you for your remembrance of me and I sincerely hope that I shall be able to thank you once more personally next summer, as I hope to meet you again in Balholm. Your painting has been admired by all who have seen it, and will fill the best place in my room. It will be doubly precious to me as a "souvenir" of you and also of the beautiful Sogne Fjord that I like so much.

Thanking you once more for your very kind gift, believe me, dear Sir, most truly yours,

Prince Boris B. Scherbatow"

The Evening Meal, 1897

While baby is asleep, 1897

Considering that princes were two a penny in pre-revolutionary Russia, and that Norway was within handy distance from St Petersburg for holiday travel, Alfred might have been in expectation of commissions. Presenting paintings as gifts to important people to impress and encourage further commissions was a common method of self-advertisement which Alfred practised on several occasions.

Mathilde found that she was expecting another baby and on their return to England the family moved to a beautiful old cottage with an orchard garden in a small hamlet outside Coniston called Haws Bank. It was here in 1900 that Frithjof was born, named after the early Norse hero of Sogn who figured in Tegner's Saga.

Alfred's work over the next two or three years was predominantly Lakeland landscape, mostly watercolours but sometimes oil. Some of his commissions involved painting a view or valley from one particular place; and he began to venture higher up the fells, though he disliked rock climbing and never attempted more than the odd scramble to reach his pitch. He worked swiftly, aiming to finish each painting in one session; but the changing weather and light often prevented this, and notes were scribbled on rough sketches so that work could be completed in his studio. Sometimes he seemed to travel round the district on "spec", searching out suitable subjects and places to paint for the summer ahead, or the autumn. He started to experiment with pastels, colouring his sketches crudely, but effectively. These pastels may only have been intended as a rough colour guide for studio painting later, but that has not discouraged Alfred's admirers from buying the small sketches as finished works in their own right.

The family increased again in 1903 with the birth of William, often called Heaton by his close friends. More space had to be found. The house Alfred chose was much nearer the centre of Coniston, just a short walk down the

Rydal Water

lane from the village. The Gate House, by Mines Beck, was soon re-named *Solheim*, or Sunny Home by Alfred. It is situated near the gates of Holywath, the old Coniston manor house.

The couple and their three children returned to Norway for three months in the summer of 1904, where Alfred worked as usual. The long hours of daylight were perfect for his *en plein air* style of painting, and he looked less at the people around him working, and more towards the distant fjords and mountains.

It was on such a day in 1904 that an event so important happened that it changed Alfred's life. The event in question was a knock on the door at *Solheim*, and the caller was from the London publishers, A & C Black. Mathilde was nursing William when the representative arrived to offer Alfred a commission. Alfred was actually out painting, but Ellide must have known where. She was sent to find her daddy, and brought him back at once.

Solheim, Coniston, 1904 (now The Gate House)

Blacks were producing a series of popular guide books at a price ordinary people could afford, and they were looking for suitable illustrators. In the absence of colour photography, water colour paintings were to be reproduced to illustrate the books. A large book about the English Lakes was planned for the following year to be written by the journalist, W T Palmer. Blacks asked Alfred if he would produce 75 paintings, for the price of £3 each. This fee included the surrender of the copyright, but Alfred was so delighted at the size of the commission that he didn't question the arrangement, and Blacks subsequently reproduced the same paintings several times with each re-print of the book, without paying Alfred any royalties.

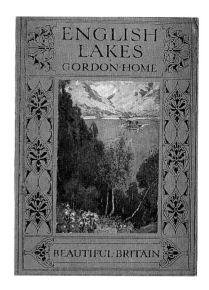

Alfred felt his luck had changed and he had found success and fortune at last. But he had no studio in Coniston from which to project himself and his work. Although the artist, art critic, socialist philosopher and philanthropist John Ruskin had been dead some four years his fame continued to attract a steady stream of visitors to Coniston and Brantwood. Riding, as it were, on the back of this local attraction, Alfred, the painter, illustrator and writer decided he needed a place to which he could invite the public to a permanent exhibition - a building where he could both paint and sell paintings.

If Alfred were to apply for planning permission today to import and erect a distinctively Norwegian red-painted wooden log cabin in the middle of Coniston, the opposition would cause a furore. Planners would refuse it on the grounds that it would look out of character surrounded by Westmorland green slate. But fortunately for Alfred, planning committees had yet to be invented and his cabin was ordered, from Jakob of Trondheim.

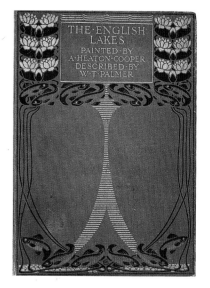

To Alfred's surprise, the cost of transporting it from Newcastle to Coniston far exceeded the price of the building itself. It had a distinctive red roof, and was decorated with carved Viking dragon heads. Each plank was carefully numbered and had to be assembled in exactly the right order and its first resting-place in England was behind The Crown Hotel, in the garden of a cafe called Mr Mandle's Restaurant.

Coniston suddenly had a new artist, competing for attention with his brash new studio - and his arrival brought consternation and competition to the Ruskinites. Not everybody entirely welcomed Alfred's rather public presence. In addition to this, it would seem that Alfred voiced some sort of antagonism towards the art exhibitions held by W G Collingwood, Ruskin's painter friend and secretary of the Ruskin Institute, as unwelcome competition. The failure, so far, of the august Lake Artists Society to invite Alfred to join them as a member also offended him, and things came to a head in July, 1905, when an article printed in *The Sphere* quoted allusions made by Collingwood to Alfred's monopolistic attitude. The remarks, which Collingwood insisted were meant as a compliment, were mischievously misinterpreted by the writer of the article, who referred to Alfred and Collingwood as gamecocks, made to fight for the amusement of trippers.

Books illustrated by Alfred for A&C Black

Coniston (with the new studio in red) 1905

The 'Norwegian' studio, Coniston, 1907

Collingwood wrote to Alfred to apologise:

Dear Mr Cooper,

I am sorry there has been this silly allusion to us in a newspaper, because the intended compliment to you - which would have been just and useful, if it had stood alone - is spoiled by the obvious ignorance or malevolence of the writer. Not that it matters in any other way, because plenty of people can prove the criticism isn't true; and as for mere press attacks, I am hardened to them, and never found the least good or harm result to me from anything printed in a paper.

But I don't like the suggestion that you and I are to be considered as the Coniston gamecocks, made to fight for the amusement of trippers. For my part, I don't admit the insinuation that I am fighting you - even to the extent of competing by exhibition. Holding some sort of show was always the plan of the Institute, and we held many before you came here. Next year we propose an arts and crafts exhibition; this thing will carry on longer than either you or I: it is no antagonism to your studio, but really an additional interest to the visitor, who in this way hears of Coniston as an art-centre and comes here prepared to see pictures. The Lakes Artists Society is a very old idea and seems to have caught on. Several of the members have their own shows, like you, but still don't take up a position of antagonism. Next year we propose having our exhibition at Keswick where they are building a place on purpose for us. I wish you saw your way to joining the Society, for that would be a practical answer to the problem raised by "The Sphere". Our next meeting for the election of members will be September 21st.

As in politics, the principals may be very civil and friendly in an election fight. But the rowdies on each side are not. I don't see why we should give rowdies a reason for a campaign of abuse, using our names in vain. I consider your studio, and the book that is coming out, as advantages to the district, and I now and then send people to see the one, and I shall, of course, recommend the other among local books mentioned in our antiquarian society's next transactions. This does not amount to much, but it means that I'm not trying to fight you.

But all the same, I think there are village gossips who would like to see a fight; and one can't stop their tongues except by showing them that there is no fight.

Believe me,
Yours sincerely,
W. G. Collingwood."

Alfred never did take up Collingwood's invitation to join the prestigious Lakes Artists Society. By refusing to do so, he sacrificed an opportunity to become part of the newly-founded art establishment in the district. Perhaps this was due, partly, to the huge gulf that lay between a painter such as Alfred and the talented "amateur" gentlemen of the Lake Artists. These amateurs painted for fun, not money; they lived in the big houses, and even though it was "new" money which financed their leisure, they were all well-educated, swapping Greek and Latin epithets or enjoying esoteric jokes about literature and politics.

W.G. Collingwood had been a student of John Ruskin's at Oxford, and became a close friend of the great man, eventually moving to Lanehead at Coniston to be close to Ruskin. He was a fine landscape painter himself, and a keen archaeologist and Roman historian. He was as well liked locally as Ruskin, the "Professor", had been and after Ruskin's death, the kind and thoughtful Collingwood succeeded him as Coniston's most notable resident.

Collingwood's background, education and comfortable wealth could not have contrasted more sharply with Alfred's situation. Alfred came from a poor working-class family, in an age before such humble origins were fashionable. Victorian society's judgement of a man was based largely on class and material values. Alfred might have been tolerated in an amused sort of way, but could he ever have competed socially with fellow painters in the Lake Artists Society had they known that Alfred's mother was illiterate?

Levers Water, 1900

Portrait of Ellide by
Mrs Collingwood, 1902

Would they ever have allowed him to become one of them - or would his desperate need to earn a living by selling his art have alienated him from those to whom art was amusement rather than business?

After Ruskin's death in 1900, Collingwood mounted a special exhibition at the Institute in Coniston to raise funds for an extension to the building. It was too small for all the local functions held there and Collingwood's exhibition proved such a success that there was plenty of money to build a new section on to the rear of the building. Other exhibitions followed.

No wonder Alfred, who painted for a living, resented the competition that these exhibitions posed to his permanent display at the Norwegian Log house. He relied on selling paintings to feed himself and his family; and to see wealthy amateurs sticking forty guinea sales tickets on their pictures must have appeared to Alfred as if they were taking the very bread out of his mouth.

But the situation has to be seen from both sides. Looking at it from Collingwood's point of view, Alfred may well have been viewed as a young upstart when he arrived. He had no local connections and little tradition of painting within the area. To arrive in this fashion, and then, within a couple of years or so, to import and erect an ostentatious if quaint Norwegian log cabin in the midst of a quiet Lakeland village without so much as a `by your leave` was a gesture of some arrogance and impertinence.

Furthermore, to have the gall to object to other artists holding occasional exhibitions, sometimes in aid of a good cause, did nothing to endear Alfred to any of his fellow artists. In his defence, he was probably desperately concerned to make a success of his new venture, but his behaviour had the effect of distancing him from the gentlemen painters of the Lake Artists, and he continued to distance himself from them all his life.

Perhaps, with some disdain, they regarded him as a purely commercial painter, churning out pretty landscapes to sell to visitors. It is nevertheless a pity that the matter was never amicably resolved. Membership of the Lakes Artists would have bestowed him with easy respectability and many sales over the years. Instead, he chose to stay out in the cold, just one step removed from the recognised art establishment. He paid dearly for his proud independence and principles.

So Alfred never attended the September meeting of the Lake Artists Society. Only a month after he received Collingwood's letter, he and his family left Coniston intending to live at least part of the year in Norway. He may have been influenced in his decision to settle at Balholm by the publicity that resulted from the "gamecocks of Coniston" skirmish. Or perhaps it was simply that the Blacks commission secured his future as an artist, enabling him to do what he had always wanted to do - to live in the fjords. The Lakes book commission had been completed on time and Blacks had published a special de luxe first edition of 500 large format copies, bound in white and

Flowing to the Lake, Coniston

Kitchen at the Ship Inn, Coniston, 1905

Sketch for Ship Inn Kitchen

gold with colour plates printed in Germany, each one protected by tissue paper. The book was an immediate success.

The whole family arrived in Balholm in August. Alfred wrote in his guide book:

"Sailing down the Sognefjord from the sea coast, the scenery gradually assumes wilder and grander proportions as we advance. At Vadheim it is just beginning to be interesting and attractive, and when we come to Balholm, we enter into the finest part of the fjord. Here are prosperous farms, smiling orchards and waving cornfields and as an effective contrast, glacier and snowfield crown the high and steep mountains around."

Norwegian artists liked to live in traditional wooden houses, preferably by a fjord, and Alfred was no exception. A house similar to the new Coniston studio was erected, though it was a bigger building with two storeys, and bedrooms upstairs. It was called *Cooperhus* and provided both a home and studio for the the family. The family's own rowing boat was tied up at the water's edge outside.

Alfred and family at home in Norway, 1906

It was a golden time for the young Heaton Coopers, as William remembered:

"I was about three or four then, and we had very good Christmas parties, and we loved dressing up and going and calling on people. In mid-winter everyone went about on skis, even the children had skis, very simple flat boards just chamfered up at the end and we slipped about in the village or anywhere with these home-made skis.

"...I was only three when I saw somebody in my father's clothes and then I found it was my aunt, I couldn't work this out at all. I was really terrified something had changed! They loved dressing up.

"...It was so natural because everyone else spoke Norwegian and I

remember we had to learn English when we came back to England, we'd forgotten our English!

"It was a very happy time... this tiny family in this village, we became very much one family at Christmas. And the church was across the fjord so on Sunday mornings we had a very gay procession of boats and the women with all their local dress with beaded fronts and the married women wearing a hat called a scaut which stuck out on both sides... and we got across Ese Fjord, and there was a path through the fields up to the church. The church itself was very charming, it had mostly glass, clear glass round the sides and as you sat in the pew you could look across the fjord and see the weather and fells and everything; the parson had so many parishes to look after, he could only come every third Sunday, so he gave a sermon three times as long as usual! And the farmers used to come in with their dogs, which would lie under the pew, then the men would go out and sell a cow or flock of sheep and discuss the year together, and when they came back the sermon was still going on!

"My father was out every possible day, and sometimes when it was really quite hard weather he would go out and make little sketches in pencil and then come back and paint them with the colour, from memory. He had a very good colour memory.

"... it was very exciting when he came back to show us what he'd brought back in the bag and we were all very critical of it too, and told him when he wasn't so good."

Dressing up. (left to right) Mathilde, Ellide, Frithjof and William, 1907

The growing importance of Balholm as a tourist centre was emphasised by the patronage of the Norwegian Royal family themselves with a visit from King Haakon, Queen Maud and Crown Prince Olav, who was, by co-incidence, dressed for the occasion in an identical reindeer skin suit to the young William's. But despite the wealth of rich and famous visitors, after fifteen months, lack of finances once again forced Alfred to leave Norway. Mathilde loved him so loyally, she would have followed him anywhere. William recalled:

"It was really a love match. They loved each other the whole of their lives together, right from the beginning. My father was the centre of her world, and the family, of course. She was just willing to follow him to any part of the world that he went. She might have missed the Norwegian summers and springs at first but many years later, I asked her if she would have liked to have stayed in Norway. She said, 'No, I would much rather live in England', so she became an Anglophile, really",

The Cooperhus now

The attempt to live in both Norway and England had been a failure:

"I think my father had the idea that he would spend spring and autumn in England and spend the summer in Balholm and have two houses in two different countries. But as usual he was very enterprising and very optimistic and that didn't quite work out. He only went back to our family home in Norway once. We stayed for 18 months and after that he found that he couldn't afford to have two homes. Bringing up a family from the income that painting alone brought was quite a battle, really, in those days."

The Cooperhus was eventually sold to Kvikne's Hotel, who still use it as an annexe; people staying there today, ninety years later, often wonder why it is still called Cooperhus. Their question can be answered by a visit to the special English room in Kvikne's where Alfred's paintings are hung with pride, alongside paintings presented for the special room by his son William and grandson Julian. Balholm left its mark on Alfred - but no greater mark than Alfred himself left on Balholm.

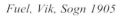

Fuel, Vik, Sogn 1905

Coniston Fells at Dawn, 1904

Chapter Five

Painter and Provider

1906-1920

It was in October 1906 that the Heaton Coopers returned to Solheim, the house they had left in Coniston fifteen months before. Family life was happy and uncomplicated because Alfred had only two major considerations in life - his art and his family. William said:

"The one thing he lived for was single-mindedly, to be a good painter, and besides the love of his family, that was the over-riding motive in his life. He was very single-minded and without guile - he was a man who was very clear and transparent and spontaneous in his friendships, too. The first memory I have of him was when I was very, very tiny, just learning to walk, and I remember this wonderful smell of tobacco, his pouch of pipe tobacco in his pocket I suppose. He was the only person I had ever met who had this wonderful smell. It was really through my nose I knew him first!

"He left most of the upbringing of us children to my mother. She was the one who ran the home and did everything. He had quite a struggle to earn a living, painting alone."

Although Alfred very rarely disciplined the children, or even told them off, they respected his authority and never disobeyed him:

"I remember him taking us bathing in Coniston Lake; I was quite small. The smell - the early morning bathe... there seemed to be a dank and fishy smell, very cold water and no sun! Horrible experience but we were quite impressed by the way my father just waded right in and started swimming. We had to go in. We never dared disobey my father, certainly, but my mother, quite often I think."

The only time the children ever noticed any disharmony between Alfred and Mathilde was when they discussed their financial problems. Shortage of money was the only thing they ever argued about, but these arguments made a great impact on William, in particular, in contrast to the usual atmosphere of peace and content. To hear his parents talking in raised voices to each other behind a closed door frightened the little boy so much that he vowed he would never worry about money in the same way when he grew up:

"They always had a hard time making ends meet, it never ended. As long as I remember there was always this worry about how we were going to pay for the meat at the butcher's, or the coal - and they talked about it, they were really very worried about money. Far too much worrying went on and it was at that time that I decided that I was never, never going to worry about money. It was so boring, always having to worry."

It was much more usual then than now for barter to take place and in this

Alfred was no exception. One former Coniston resident still possesses two pictures by Alfred, who painted them for his grandfather, the local tailor, in return for a suit of clothes.

Fathers in those days were not expected to help around the house or with the children. Alfred bought books for the children - but he didn't read to them. There were family walks up Coniston Old Man, when young William would look wistfully southwards from the summit and long for a pony to carry him at a gallop down the "wretched steep mountain" off to exciting Barrow. Alfred took his family by train to Barrow on days out and shopping trips, but chiefly to enjoy the excitement of the shipyards, where the first submarines were being built and where the children spotted foreign ships in port from as far away as Brazil.

Ellide was ten by now, and Alfred decided to move the family to Ulverston so the children could go to good secondary schools there, because education in Coniston did not extend much beyond primary level. The home they rented was one third of a fine Georgian house in Princes Street which the family called Mayfield. Four-year-old William went to a preparatory school in Church Walk and shared a bedroom with his elder brother, Frithjof, ('Fritters') who had a gift for telling stories:

"Frithjof was a delightful person, he was a very good companion even though he was three years older than me. He had that wonderful sense of telling a story - in Ulverston our bedroom window at the back of the house looked on to a churchyard and a chestnut tree, which had little pyramids of white blossom in spring. I remember Frithjof telling me that those were the ghosts of clergy who'd died there, and I believed everything he said!"

The chestnut tree is still there in the churchyard at the back of Mayfield, as weighted down with conkers each autumn as it must have been eighty years ago when Alfred's children swung from its boughs.

Each day Alfred travelled by train to Coniston to work in the studio, choosing occasionally to walk the fourteen miles journey. In 1907, Blacks published *The Norwegian Fjords*, the book that Alfred had taken fifteen years to research. His writing skills gave him far less pleasure than painting, as William remembered vividly:

"When my father had written the book in long hand script, with all these notes on where he'd been, I had to read it out and he wrote it out in long hand to send to the publishers. One day he said to me, 'You know, I'll never, never take on writing another book!' He concentrated on painting rather than writing, he was very humble about his writing gifts."

The Isle of Wight was Alfred's next commission from Blacks, followed a year later by *The Isle of Man*. Most of these books were in one of two series - the *7/6d* series, and the *"Beautiful Britain"* series. Many were re-printed several times, sometimes without acknowledgement of Alfred's illustrations. Sometimes new pictures were added to new editions. A commission for a

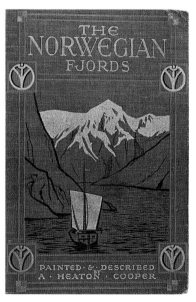

Book "The Norwegian Fjords"

Coniston from How Head, 1898

book about Norfolk or the Isle of Wight generally took Alfred away from home for at least two or three weeks at a time, and he was rarely in the house at all when he was at home because he was either out painting on the fells or in the studio. Mathilde became pregnant again in 1907, and the couple's last child, Una, was born in 1908. Mathilde needed help in the house with the four children and it was while the family lived in Ulverston that she was joined in England by one of her sisters, Otalia. The children loved their Auntie Otalia; she was very tolerant of them, and being stone deaf she was oblivious of their noise. She stayed in the Lake District for the rest of her life, though she eventually moved to Langdale to live alone after all the children had left home.

In 1911, Alfred's father, William died and was buried beside Alice and baby Rachel in the churchyard at St Peter's, Halliwell. It was Alfred's responsibility to help administer his father's estate, which wasn't easy because his brothers and sister had settled so far from home. John had become a groom, and emigrated to Brisbane, Australia; Edith had married Jean Gautreau, the regional editor of a French newspaper and lived in France; Daniel and Tom were both living in America and William may have remained in Bolton, but no trace or mention of him was ever found in family documents.

William senior's death was followed a year later by the death of his brother, Thomas Cooper, Alfred's uncle, who had been a well-respected member of Bolton's business community. Thomas's daughter, Nellie, had found fame and fortune by marrying a Frenchman, Pierre Wibaux, dubbed locally as *"The Cattle King of Montana."* The couple had emigrated to Montana as prospectors and Pierre become immensely successful as a stock rearer and cattleman. Their meteoric rise from pioneer mud hut in Montana to an elegant mansion, with winter homes in California and Paris, attracted much attention in Nellie's native Bolton, and the Wibaux featured in a delightful article in the *Bolton Daily News* in 1895 headed *The Cattle King of Montana - A Boltonian 'At Home'*

Perhaps such fame and success caused family jealousy; and Thomas's funeral, far from being a family re-union for Nellie Wibaux and her cousins Alfred, Edith, Tom and Daniel seems instead to have provoked a rift. Edith felt that the rich and famous Nellie was given far too much prominence and when she wrote to complain to Nellie that her brothers Tom and Daniel had been slighted at the funeral, Nellie was very upset indeed, and addressed her reply to Alfred, with whom she was on good terms. Alfred, being the kind and polite person that he was, and the eldest too, would certainly have tried to pour oil on troubled waters. This is what Nellie wrote from her fashionable Paris address:

"Dear Alfred,

I received this morning a letter from your sister in which she tells me that her brothers were slighted in some way at my father's funeral. I am very much surprised to hear of this - Mr Pearce, who very kindly undertook absolutely everything for me, taking upon himself all responsibility, sending out all invitations and even indicating to me how I should attend the funeral, placing my carriage in the side street - certainly did nothing to slight anyone, I am sure.

Tom and Daniel came to see me at a very painful moment just as I was leaving Halliwell Lodge - I was very much upset and really do not quite remember what was said. I think, tho, I thanked you for your letter, I am sure I thanked you for having come so far to attend the funeral. I do not wish to speak of this to Mr Pearce, he has been so kind and has done so much for me and he would, I am sure, be distressed. I therefore wish you to accept my apologies for any seeming slight. I do not quite understand why your sister should have chosen this time to claim her cousinship and write to me in these bitterest terms. If it is her intention to convey to me other meaning than the very words of her letter I wish YOU will write to me and explain.

I shall not reply to her - it is useless to renew an acquaintance under the circumstances. A very short time before Father's death she sent me a book of yours on the English Lakes. Did the book belong to them or was it lent to them? Thanking you ahead for your reply, and with kindest regards,

Believe me,
Yours most sincerely,
Nellie Wibaux
January 25th 1912

Bristol from Clifton Observatory

Porlock Church

Edith and husband,
Jean B. Gautreau

Ullswater, the Silver Strand, 1904

Windermere Station, 1907

Later that year, Alfred decided that he and the family should move house again and settle in Ambleside. He found the daily journey from Ulverston to the Coniston studio irksome, but there were other reasons. Tourism was increasing every year. Thousands of visitors arrived by train at Windermere Station, cruised up the lake, visited Ambleside, and continued on their Lakeland journey to Keswick. Ambleside and Windermere were at the very centre of the tourist trade and attracted all types of visitor - the day trippers, those who came to stay for a week or so, and those who took cottages for longer periods during the holiday season. Coniston, despite the attraction of Coniston Water with its elegant steam yachts, could never compete for sheer numbers with Windermere and Ambleside although the Furness Railway ran a regular service which terminated at Coniston. The numbers of people coming to find Ruskin memorabilia had declined as the years passed since his death, and Alfred recognised that he would sell far more paintings if his studio were situated in Ambleside. Schools for the children were suitable, too, and the town had recently been endowed with the excellent new Kelsick Grammar School.

Alfred found a family house in Millans Park, Ambleside, which looked over green fields to the fells beyond. It was a large and pleasant house called Borlands (since renamed) and suited the family well. But Alfred also wanted his Norwegian studio transported from Coniston, and re-erected in a plot of land he rented on the Lake Road corner of Wansfell Road. Moving one's wooden cabin in Norway to a new site was not unheard of, and Alfred duly arranged for it to be dismantled, carted over to Ambleside, and re-built, plank by numbered plank.

Alfred's illustrations for A & C Black's guide books continued to appear regularly, though some of them were second and third editions of books that he had illustrated a few years before. Occasionally Blacks commissioned a new writer to produce a book about an area, but illustrated with old paintings Alfred had completed for previous books. He continued to accept a flat payment for each picture commissioned, but with no royalties for continued re-use. In 1912 there was a new book by W G Clarke about Norfolk and Suffolk, and in 1915 Alfred went to Ireland to illustrate a book by Frank Mathew. Much as he enjoyed travelling round and visiting these attractive locations, he could spare very little time away from home; he had to keep his studio well stocked with Lakeland landscapes.

Purists will be surprised and perhaps a little shocked to discover that Alfred sometimes purchased postcards of the places he was asked to paint. Occasionally he made notes on the card itself, and it is obvious that he was using them as a guide to the painting he would produce or finish back at home. Given his impressive powers of recording fine detail, and his skill as an *en plein air* artist, he would have no earthly need to copy from postcards, except to meet a time deadline - this can be the only explanation for an artist of Alfred's calibre to use such a device.

It was often necessary for Alfred to be away from home for short periods even when he was painting in the Lake District. He would plan to paint in one particular area and if it was too far to travel home on foot in the evening,

Irish cottage interior, Achill Island, 1915

there were farms that he stayed at regularly. In Ullswater, it was at the Wilson's of Glencoyne; when he spent a week in Wasdale, he would be put up at the Wilson's of Burnthwaite. He got to know all the local farmers, and was very popular among them, and himself became a well-known Lakeland character. When time permitted, he enjoyed a day's hunting with the Coniston Foxhounds, and he never missed Mayor Making day at Troutbeck, when he saw all his old farming friends.

Alfred's method of working had changed considerably over the last twenty years. As he became more experienced and accomplished, he

Postcard of Oslo, used as an aid for Alfreds watercolour (below)

Oslo, Karl Johan Street, 1926

Horning, Norfolk Broads, 1919

Old Elvet Bridge, Durham

dispensed with the need for great detail in his sketching, relying instead far more on his memory. William recalls:

"He depended on his memory, visual memory, he didn't need to make notes. Occasionally in sketch books there were notes but usually it was just a pencil sketch and his own memory.

"... he once said that the mark of a good painter is the tone values as well as the colour. If you have those values correct and balanced, that shows that you have been observing and imbibing the mood of the day, He very often found that one day had a different mood from the next one and he was very sensitive to that and it came out in his work.

"I think he aimed always to start and finish on the spot, while the thing was fresh in his mind, and while the effect was still there. But of course, in England, especially when there are clouds about, and in the Lake District especially too, you can't copy what is there because it's not there any longer by the time you've mixed the colour on your paintbox and started applying it, there's an entirely different effect. So it means trusting your memory very

*Cottage interior,
Glencoyne farm, Ullswater*

Shaftesbury, Gold Hill, 1925

much more than one realises... my father, I think he would much prefer painting out of doors. Even though it had changed he would interpret the landscape, use the landscape that was there, to interpret and change it into the mood in which he first was attracted to it, and that was why he had this freshness - also a good circulation because he didn't seem to know when the wind was being rather unmerciful!"

Alfred's early love of Norway influenced his painting throughout his life. This is how he had described a night in June in *The Norwegian Fjords*:

Coniston Hunt - Red Screes, 1920

"The nearer mountains are in purple shadow. In one short hour the light on each ruddy top dies away and their colour is slowly transformed to that of cold, silvery blue as they are one by one deserted by the sun's rays. All the peaks are now of blue, purple and silver - cool and refreshing to look upon. Hardly has the last mountain taken on his silvery hue when a light zephyr breathes softly across the sleeping waters of the fjord in a steely glitter. But what is this weird light that is stealing over all Nature in softest and most delicate blush when we expected the cool twilight? It is the afterglow. An ethereal rosy golden light slowly intensifies on the mountains. It is more diffused than the actual direct glow from the setting sun, and not nearly so brilliant; but a dreamy glow, mysterious and bewitchingly weird in the intense stillness."

Time and again, there is evidence of that "afterglow" in his watercolour landscapes; even the bluest sky has the very subtlest suggestion of pink. According to William:

"He would choose what he painted by the colour of the day - for instance today, the lightest part of the whole landscape is the clouds, they had this pinky glow, so Father would take a brush full of light red or cadmium and vermilion and take it over the whole of the paper so that it shone through - he would do it like a wash to start with, let it dry, then paint on top of it, then

Ullswater, stormy day

Rydal Valley (pastel sketch), 1913

Smithy Brow, Ambleside

any blues that came on it would have this sort of warm blue, broken blue. In watercolours one gets this transparency which influences all the other colours that come on to it. I think he must have learnt a lot in Norway, certainly in the midsummer with the midnight sun."

When Alfred painted in oils, the whole procedure required more equipment and much more preparation and time, and was a very difficult medium to use for outdoor landscape painting. Alfred's grandson, Julian, a painter himself, was able to explain the problems Alfred would have had with the materials which were available in his day, and how he overcame these problems:

"Alfred had a range of hog hair brushes of different shapes and sizes, for example flat, filbert and round shaped. These last two tend to apply the paint thicker than a flat brush.

The "support" is the material on which the painting is done; I have noticed that when Alfred was using oils outside, he glued or pinned a primed piece of canvas onto a board of wood or hardboard. On other occasions, he used ready-stretched and primed canvases on stretchers, which he would have bought at an art equipment shop.

The Shepherd, Coniston, 1903

Alfred's oil palette

He may sometimes have done the odd oil sketch on a piece of cardboard or hardboard lying around, in which case he would size it first with rabbit skin glue or the equivalent, and then prime it with lead white. The trouble with this is that it takes two or three weeks for the white to dry - and it needed two coats. Nowadays two coats of acrylic white can be ready in an hour.

The "medium" is the binding agent for the powder colour. Oil must produce a good working consistency and also harden in a convenient length of time on exposure to air. Linseed oil (cold pressed) is the oil which Alfred probably used. Alfred would not have needed to add much oil - a certain amount comes in the paint from the tube: for his way of direct, fairly gestural painting, the paint consistency needs to have a certain stiffness to it.

The "thinner" used is turpentine. For the correct sequence in oil painting, "lean to fat", it is necessary to thin with the turpentine in the early stages of the painting - unless the painting is going to be completed in one session, with no underpainting. This would apply to Alfred's outdoor oils.

As a landscape painter, the range of colours Alfred would have used included the earth colours, so called because they are made, quite literally, from the earth of different regions in Italy. His choice of colours was raw umber, burnt umber, raw and burnt sienna, venetian red, naples yellow, terre verte. He had three blues - cobalt, ultramarine and prussian blue. His greens would probably have been terre verte and viridian, but often he would prefer to make his own green, out of yellows and blues. He also used light red and cadmium red, which was very expensive and rarely needed, and alizarin crimson. His yellows were yellow ochre and lemon yellow and for white he had flake white, which is creamy and heavy, and zinc white, which was silvery and transparent and excellent for Alfred's skies and water. He wouldn't have used black at all.

We still have some of Alfred's palettes; there is a big oval one for the studio, but the others are smaller and rectangular. He probably carried everything in a special wooden equipment box, including the palette in the box lid. He had a folding easel, which he also used for watercolour painting, and in the studio he had a larger easel, with a ratchet and handle for moving it up or down."

The whole concept of direct painting from nature was relatively new when Alfred decided to adopt it as his *modus operandi*; even now it poses many practical problems, but there were many more in Alfred's day, using less sophisticated materials:

Sogn, Fjaerlands, 1906

"Ideally, direct painting should express a single mood at a single sitting. There is no technical objection to this if the paint is put on in one 'go' and is then left to dry undisturbed. But direct painting is a recent innovation for landscape. It was not really practicable until the introduction, in the nineteenth century, of paint manufactured in tubes.

...by working on the spot in the heat of direct inspiration from nature, the Impressionists produced landscapes that are so fresh in vision and so apparently instantaneous in handling that we may be tempted to think, 'This is the only way to paint' But we would be wrong."

In his excellent chapter on the advantages and disadvantages of "direct painting" in his book *Preparation For Painting*, Lynton Lamb listed many of the problems, challenges and experiences Alfred would have encountered. Painting outside is often:

"Physically irksome and mentally frustrating; equipment is heavy and usually has to be carried some distance from the nearest road; the weather will probably change as the painter works through the day, the light certainly will. The glare from the sun may blind him and make colour accuracy impossible,

Tjugum village, 1891

Hopfield, Kent, 1895

and if he seeks the shade, everything appears green under the leafy trees. Summer is the most practical time for out of doors painting, but some of the best landscapes can be found in winter, when the cold or the wind and rain make it impossible to work outside. With problems such as these, can 'direct painting' ever be possible? Or can a compromise be found?

"Because the art of landscape painting does not consist of mere transcriptions of scenery, pictures need not be made in the open air..."

Lamb concluded:

"Even Degas, who was an Impressionist, firmly rejected the idea that an outdoor scene must be painted on the spot. He said, 'La peinture n'est pas du sport'. And that is just it... 'The art of oil painting in its excellence,' says Sickert, 'demands execution in several stages, with, in Northern climates, long intervals for drying'. The serious artist, therefore, will want to find some way in which he can work continuously without disturbance. It is possible to combine direct and indirect painting."

This is exactly what Alfred discovered, and once he had made this discovery, he worked out his own compromise. Sometimes, in good weather, he worked out of doors in watercolours or oils, coming closest to the *plein air* ideal; other times, he sketched for short periods in oil, or pastels, or made a drawing with notes to indicate which colours he would use when the drawing became a painting. Then, having made the first "direct" contact with nature, he moved back indoors to finish the picture.

This is how Julian visualises his grandfather at work out of doors:

"For his outdoor oils, Alfred would walk to the spot he had chosen, which would be away from the likely passage of people, and set up his easel. He would put a ring of all the colours he thought might be used round the edge of the palette, pour out some turpentine into a little metal container which might hang from the easel on a string, and start drawing in the landscape with cobalt blue or ultramarine, thinned down with the turps, until he had got the main masses of mountains and proportions of sky and foreground worked out.

Then he would start straight in, painting distant mountain or land first, coming closer to the foreground, intensifying colour and deepening dark tones in relation to nearness. Then to the sky - having been observing it moving whilst painting, he would either choose to paint in what was happening at that moment, or a better sequence of clouds and light from up to an hour ago, using a combination of memory and observation.

Then he might be able to relax a little and stand back and have a smoke, because the anxiety of getting down something constantly changing and alive is considerable, particularly without a camera. Having got essentially everything down in front of his eyes that he wanted, adjusting positions and shapes as he went along, he could then start to fill out details in the foreground, put in a figure or a boat, or adjust or accentuate a colour, until time passing has made the actual landscape change too much.

With the influence of French Impressionists and other 19th century 'plein air' painters on him, Alfred used fairly strong colour both in the light and through the shadows, not relying on tonal changes solely."

The oil paintings done in the studio were taken at a much more leisurely pace:

"These studio oils would use drawings, watercolour, pastel or oil sketches as a basis, and the canvas would be on a stretcher and taken much more slowly, with underpainting allowed to dry a day or two before the next layer. There was time to fine tune compositional arrangements and to have changes of mind. Alfred's impetus in his studio painting was to take further something not quite fully realised on the spot."

These fuller, more carefully painted oils were not only more exhibitable, but more expensive, too, and would have been the sort of pictures Alfred sent to Bromley's in Bolton, or to the Royal Academy.

One reason why Alfred's work was largely concentrated on the Lake District for several years was the first World War, which restricted his travel and made it impossible to visit Europe, and Norway in particular.

Mathilde had developed painful arthritis, and found it increasingly difficult to get out and about with Alfred. Occasionally he would take the four children with him for the day to give Mathilde and Aunt Otalia a rest. William recalled:

"I remember going to Elterwater Common because my father sat there for hours and hours and we knew that we were free to just enjoy ourselves and we footled round exploring the little streams and pools and finding creatures, water beetles and things. I remember coming across some fresh water shrimps at one time. And the smell of myrtle...

"We were never allowed to interrupt Father to show him the things we had found. He would forget all about us - absolutely right of course! We'd always picnic and spend these long summer days just playing around."

The family had moved yet again, this time to the gardener's cottage at the back of Rothay Manor, near the bridge over the Rothay at Ambleside. The Manor was owned by Sir George and Lady McKay, a wealthy but rather lonely elderly couple whose lavish and often impromptu parties were legendary. Sir George was an entrepreneur who had made his money out west in Canada and America and was always urging the young William to *"Go out and live like a man!"* Lady McKay was Austrian but had been banished from Austria because her father had been involved in the murder of a crown prince, as recounted in *The Prisoner of Zenda*. The couple welcomed the company of Alfred and Mathilde next door, and the McKays and the Heaton Coopers spent many evenings together playing bridge, a pleasure which continued long after the Heaton Coopers had moved yet again and the two families were no longer neighbours.

After the war started in 1914, Alfred joined the Local Defence Volunteers, which was a fore-runner to the Home Guard. This early version of Dad's Army didn't have uniforms, but they did have rifles, much to the children's

Langdale Pikes from Oak Howe Farm

Wood Farm, Troutbeck

delight and Alfred spent many an evening in the park, stabbing at sandbags with his bayonet, or practising on the Loughrigg rifle range up near the old golf course. He was sociable at all times, and got on well with his fellow men.

There was little visible sign of war in Ambleside except at the beginning of hostilities when horses queued night and day to be shoed at the smithy in The Slack before being sent to France. One or two fields were requisitioned on the outskirts of the village for army transit camps, but there was little that ordinary people could do to help the war effort, except knit socks for the soldiers and wait anxiously for news from the Front. It was during the war that many local families first began to take a daily newspaper to scan the lists of those who had fallen, instead of relying on the one copy in the local reading room or working mens' institute. The war itself seemed very remote to the people of Westmorland, isolated as they were from any action. Most country people were virtually self sufficient in food, and supplied others who were not, avoiding food shortages. Life went calmly on in spite of the tragedies which struck individual families when sons were killed.

Alfred's household was a busy one, with the four children growing up and bringing their friends to the house and studio. Ellide was a frequent visitor

Frithjof, 1918

Ellide marries Harold Carson Parker, pictured at the Log House studio, Ambleside, 1917

to the Carson Parker family at Springfield, Rydal Road. During the War years, she left home for a while to do war work on the East Coast, but married into the family in 1917.

Frithjof, who had grown up to be a calm, steady youth, was apprenticed as an engineer for five years to W Fell & Co, four miles away at Troutbeck Bridge. But his patriotic urge to serve his country led him to lie about his age, and he signed up at only 17 years old to serve with the Royal Flying Corps. He came home, wounded, at the end of the war.

William was still at Kelswick Grammar School, and Una at Charlotte Mason College's prototype PNEU (Parents' National Educational Union) school at Fairfield, when they became very friendly with the MacIver children.

The MacIver family of eight children lived first in Windermere, and then moved to Ambleside, quite near to their maternal grandmother MacIver, who presided over her large family from the splendour of Wanlass Howe (better known nowadays as Ambleside Park), a big Victorian house at Waterhead. The house had gardens which ran down to the water's edge, where she kept her boats. The grandchildren and their friends, particularly the Heaton Coopers, made full use of the garden and the lake and spent many hours together; and when they weren't playing at grandmother MacIver's, the children could be found almost any time at Alfred's studio. The quaint wooden building held enormous fascination for them; there was nothing else quite so extraordinary in the whole of Ambleside. Just to step inside the studio, with its walls crowded with hundreds of colourful paintings was like entering Aladdin's cave.

Both Alfred and Mathilde welcomed the children as if they were part of the family; one of the little girls was Joan MacIver (later Mrs Joan Cottam) who never forgot the warmth and affection of life with the Heaton Coopers:

"We were all very fond of Alfred. He was a most kind man, I never heard him cross, I never saw him looking anything but extremely good natured and friendly to all of us. I don't think we were exactly a nuisance but we clearly interfered with his work and he always appeared to be very happy to see us and spend a lot of his time with us in the studio. If we hadn't been there, he would have been doing a bit of work on one of his pictures.

"He used to go out on the fells, take sketch books and make rough notes about colours and things like that on the pad -

and then when he came back he'd put all the finishing touches to the main picture which was in the studio.

"We would spend hours there - we would look at the paintings and ask about them and talk about them as if we might be interested in buying them. I think he was quite pleased to have someone to talk to and tell about his pictures and we were very interested. We would watch him mixing his colours and ask him what colour he was going to use for this or that, and then he would be quite pleased to tell us. He was painting mostly in oils but when he went sketching it was probably watercolours because oils wouldn't dry, you couldn't put it in your knapsack over your shoulder - it might get rained on. I think all he did in the studio was almost entirely oils.

"He was very patient, I don't know if he thought we were taking it all in. I think we were conscious that we were interrupting him and didn't want to push him too far. He always had such a lovely welcome for us. We would have been very sad if he'd said 'Oh now, look here, that's enough now, off you go,' but he never ever said that. He always said, 'Oh, hello!' and greeted us as if he was pleased to see us. I think he was; I think he had a love of children.

"Mathilde was never annoyed by this attention. She almost accepted us as part of her family. She was always pleased that we went to see her - she couldn't move about much. She didn't show people round, she just sort of sat in the studio. They had a saucer - there was no admission charge that I remember, and people could put money in if they wanted to. There was always a large number of coppers and occasionally silver coins. Mathilde always kept an eye on them and when there was about a shilling, she would give it to Una and say, 'Go on, Una, go next door and get some cakes!' Then she'd come back and we would all eat them, they were very generous.

"I don't think they had a lot of money. His paintings didn't sell for an awful lot of money in those days. I don't suppose he sold a lot from what were on view in his studio, because I can remember my favourite one seemed to be there

Alfred and Mathilde at the Log House, 1913

Alfred, 1915

for a long time. He must have made a living, but I think it was a pretty scanty living - and they were the most generous, hospitable people, they were very nice and very kind.

"The studio walls were covered with paintings. They were all hanging in frames and occasionally, when one was sold, I don't think it was necessarily sold in the frame - then another picture would be put into that frame. If people came and asked him any questions or wanted to know about the pictures, he would leave what he was doing and talk to them and take them round. I don't ever remember a lot of people being in the studio at any one time.

"Alfred spent a lot of time actually painting on the fells, and when he wasn't in the studio, his wife would be there. And Mathilde's sister helped back at home; she was very good at cooking, and spoke pidgin English. When she said anything wrong we all used to laugh, and she would laugh too. They were always a very happy family, I can never remember them being anything but happy.

"Alfred was really genial to look at, we were very fond of him and regarded him as a friend. He was always well dressed, he usually had a bright coloured waistcoat and red tie and he had fairly long hair, latterly it was white hair and he was rather like Mr Pickwick! He always looked dressed in the country tradition and he always had a gay waistcoat, perhaps made by the Norwegian aunt or his wife. He always looked picturesque, the waistcoat was red or yellow, always a cheerful colour. It blended in with the studio, he dressed as an artist and he looked the part. His general knowledge was good, and the spoken word excellent and from that I got the impression that he must have been well-educated, perhaps at a grammar school and then college."

Alfred enjoyed the bustle of family life back at home, but without actually taking a major role in affairs:

"He would come back from the studio and sit in his chair. I think he used to smoke a pipe and he would sit there quietly reflecting and probably thinking about what he'd been doing

on the fells. He was almost like part of the furniture, he just sat there, quite happy. He didn't sit there and fall asleep - he saw what was going on but he never took much part. I don't think he ever found the family too noisy, or that he would ever complain about anything. He was a really lovable character. He was a great walker - you never saw him resting his feet or saying his feet were tired; and he never seemed to feel the cold - when he came in, he wouldn't necessarily sit by the fire."

When the war ended in 1918, Alfred bought an old bell tent for the family to camp, and use for picnics. The only family portrait he ever painted was at a family picnic held outside the bell tent. The children enjoyed the tent so much, Alfred then rented an old hut for ten shillings a year from the Army near the firing range on Loughrigg Fell. He used it for shelter when he was painting in bad weather in that area, and the children used it when they were camping on Loughrigg, often for days at a time during the long school holidays. They lined it inside with bracken for their bedding, and washed up their pots and pans in the stream nearby. William recalled:

"My father rented it just to have for us children. A marvellous time we had! We had lots of friends coming and staying there with us, mostly it was during the school holidays, we just ran wild up there. We took food up and cooked it ourselves. Those were very happy days, and I thought it was very nice of my father to do that.

"He had become very fond of Loughrigg. He could climb as far as that, there was no rock climbing involved. He loved to paint from Loughrigg, you can go to different points and see new views of Langdale, little tarns, spots of water too. I think those were the happiest painting places.

Autumn Afternoon on the Rothay, Ambleside

"The hut was about a quarter to half a mile beyond the old golf course. But it wasn't on the track, it was in a valley by itself, of its own, and that's why we didn't bother anyone. When we had friends to stay, they were usually painters, student friends of mine from London and we asked them if they would leave a work of theirs in the hut, so gradually we collected quite a lot of drawings in there. And then when I was in London, I came home for the summer and found the hut had been smashed up, all the drawings had gone, the whole place smashed up. They had vandals in those days."

Una and Joan MacIver, who went to Girl Guides together, had been frequent visitors to the hut, and the close ties between the MacIvers and the Heaton Coopers continued well into adult life. When Joan grew up, she trained to be a nurse in London and decided to go to India, but not without a special keepsake from Alfred:

"He took me into the studio because he knew we were so interested in it - 'Now,' he said, 'I'd like you to take something to remind you of England. Which picture would you like?' He said it, just like that, to me! So I looked all round and I chose a lovely one of sand dunes, a beautiful oblong picture. I took it to India and it was my pride and joy."

The story had a sad ending; the ravages of the Indian climate and mildew combined with armies of paper-eating white ants eventually took their toll, and Alfred's gift, thought to have been painted off the Cumbria coast somewhere near Seascale, was reduced to shreds.

The affection that Alfred showed towards these lively and inquisitive children was reciprocated; they shared a mutual love of being in the studio surrounded by the wealth of colour and beauty which the pictures brought to the panelled walls. The impression that Alfred made on them never faded, and their recall of him was as strong as if he had been their own father. Joan's description of the genial Alfred is echoed by his son, William:

"He would have only one suit of green, speckled with orange (bracken in autumn) of the best tweed, and a loose-fitting jacket with two poacher's pockets to hold a sketch book and pencils or crayons. He wore slightly baggy britches to below the knee, and stockings to harmonize, knitted by his wife. He wore a bow tie and a hat made of tweed with a wide brim. When he was climbing to reach his subjects, he wore farmers' boots, and always used a walking stick with an iron spike on the end.

"He had a rucksack and a half imperial board that was 22 by 16 inches, and then an easel, a wooden easel strapped on top of that, and he had a stick. He would never use a stick to sit on and work, a shooting stick. He would always stand, the easel was tall enough to paint standing.

"He was by nature a sunny person, who saw life simply and as a whole. The greatest motive of his life was to be a good painter. Over the years as this aim was achieved and the children launched in life, painting well and with truth to nature became his one great aim, yet he enjoyed meeting people as long as it didn't come between him and his work. He and Mathilde loved

and respected each other for the whole of their life together - thirty five years - and this love match coloured the whole of his life. He was not one to show emotions - these came out mostly through his paintings. He had a delightful, earthy sense of humour and enjoyed telling a good yarn as well as listening to one."

One of Alfred's favourite stories that he never tired of telling was about a botanist that he had met, a Professor Ball. William heard the story told many a time:

"This Professor Ball went to different parts of the world to look at different plants. He took, among other plants, some sunflowers up to the North Cape of Norway and he went to look at them late in the summer and he found all the sunflowers were dead and the flowers had dropped off. He realised that of course the sunflowers move round with the sun - and the sun never sets. So they'd choked themselves!"

Alfred also loved to hear local dialect and never forgot how one farmer answered a query from an American tourist as to whether it rained all the time in the Lake District: *"Well, it donks and it doddles, dozzles bedoes, and mebbe it cum a bit o' a stickter, but nivver what you might call a gay gurt pell!"* Alfred repeated time and again, but never without a chuckle.

Alfred had never shown a great interest in religion or church attendance throughout his life, although he was a member of the Church of England. He had always expressed his emotions and love of life through the beauty of nature which he tried so faithfully to reproduce through his paintings; and his service to God, and even his acts of worship took the form of using his God-given talents of painting to the very best of his ability. He never spoke about his beliefs or love of God to his children, but even without discussing the subject, the children understood and recognized Alfred's silent form of devotion as he strove, 'simple mindedly', to become a better painter all his life.

Haycutting, Grasmere

Launchy Ghyll, Thirlmere

However, it was when the children were growing up in Ambleside that Alfred began to express his religious feelings in a more positive form by attending church. But it wasn't the rather grand Parish Church of St Mary's, Ambleside built only fifty years before which attracted Alfred. Instead he walked each Sunday to the small but very picturesque Italianate church of Holy Trinity, Brathay, built on a small knoll above the river near Brathay footbridge on a site which Wordsworth himself had judged to be the most beautiful outside the Alps.

"Seeing God in nature had, up till now, been mainly his sort of worship. But he began to have a faith in God, much more consciously - he always had faith but I think by going to church at Brathay, that built it up into a more

Moonlight, Windermere, 1906

real sort of faith. We as children were very happy, just believing, because our parents believed, but they didn't speak about it. Alfred's favourite service was Matins, and we always used to go to Brathay rather than Ambleside because of the walk there, he always liked walking in the morning, so we had to walk there and back again. It was a very simple sort of service, and he didn't join in the parish life much."

Throughout his life, William watched his father at work, every day, drawing, sketching and painting. When William was about eleven, he began to draw and paint himself, but was a little disappointed when Alfred seemed oblivious of his youthful attempts. However, about three years later, the moment arrived when Alfred handed his son a paintbox, brushes and paper and invited him to go out painting with him.

"The very first painting, the first time that he invited me to come out with him was along the Brathay valley, just further up the stream from Brathay Church where there's a rocky bit of stream which flattens out to the meadows. It was a very difficult subject, I remember it very well. It was the river and a lot of stringy trees, scruffy little trees with lots of changes of colour. It wasn't an easy, simple landscape with lots of big washes, it was something very

Morning sun, Holme Point, Lake Windermere

difficult, but that fired me even more to go out with him, and he was very glad to have the company, I think. He didn't talk much, he just painted rather than talked about it... I can't remember a single time that he actually taught me anything. And yet he was teaching me all the time, you see, I was watching him painting and when I went out with him, he did it by his hands and eye rather than by his voice which I think was very sound, much better than anything."

Alfred spoke as little about art as he did about his personal beliefs in God, preferring, instead, to teach by silent example.

It was Alfred's early influence on William which shaped his life. At about eleven years old, William's godmother was persuaded by the vicar of Ambleside to pay for him to attend public school at St Bee's, near Whitehaven, on condition that he made a career for himself as a clergyman in the Church of England. William was coached for the entrance exam, and passed. But his real ambition was to be a painter, like his father, and the offer of a public school education was rejected. He told Alfred and Mathilde of his plans, and they were delighted, much to his surprise. Instead of St Bee's, William cycled three days a week to attend Kendal Art College. He helped Alfred in the studio by making up the log fires and helping to clean the building, eventually graduating to mounting pictures and making frames for them.

As William's own distinctive style emerged, his view of Alfred's work was not uncritical. William's painting was simpler altogether, spare and lighter in touch and detail than his father's rather heavier, more dramatic vision of nature. The more expensive the commission, the more paint Alfred thought it deserved; but this over-painting, according to William, deadened the scene the picture was trying to portray:

"In the early days, my father thought that if a painting was too sketchy, he wasn't giving his money's worth to the customer, so he conscientiously worked on and on and killed it. I often thought he worked too long on a watercolour, striving to attain the strength of an oil painting instead of allowing the white paper to show through the washes of the watercolour, but in this I could well have been mistaken, for in his best and later work, he retained both delicacy and strength.

"But I think I had quite an influence on him, I was always asking him to stop and leave it, so his work was much bolder towards the end of his life, and he was learning a lot, all his life's experience was in it then."

Alfred was always extremely co-operative towards his sponsors when somebody commissioned a painting. If a particular angle of a scene was requested, Alfred would do it as demanded, unlike William:

"Usually he would try and oblige them. I know what I would have done! I wouldn't have been dictated to, I would have done it the way I thought best at the time. He was aware of giving people their money's worth - it was his accountancy training, from his early days."

Piers Ghyll, 1923

Among Alfred's wealthiest patrons at this time was a man called William Heaton, who had made a lot of money during the war out of balloon fabric and became a millionaire. When he came to the Lakes, he would rent a very large house, such as Rydal Hall or Wray Castle or Pull Woods - and then he would ask Alfred to paint it for him. He took a great interest in Alfred's work, and he gave him commissions to paint these houses, especially Rydal Hall.

Alfred's Norwegian paintings did not sell in Ambleside as well as his Lakeland landscapes, but he did collect admirers of his Norwegian work who bought the Norway paintings, and commissioned others. Angus Watson, of the Skippers Sardine family was particularly fond of the Norwegian paintings, as mentioned in a previous chapter.

The busiest, most active period of Alfred's family life drew to a close as the children left home, one by one. 'Home' by this time was no longer the gardener's cottage, but a tall, semi-detached Victorian terraced house at the bottom of Compston Road, facing the putting green. The family brought a splash of colour to the row by painting their front door red, and from that time the house was always referred to as the 'Red Door'. It was from here that Ellide married Harold Carson Parker when she was twenty-one years old, and went to South India as the wife of a rubber planter. Ellide's wedding reception was held in the studio, and the happy couple posed for the photographs on the wooden balcony outside the studio just below the Viking dragon's head. *(See page 99)*

Then Frithjof left home after his five year's apprenticeship had expired at Fell's, Troutbeck Bridge:

"Fritters, he was entirely practical, there was none of the influence of my father, probably much more of my mother with him. After he left Fell's he went to Hayes Aircraft to the west of London, at Hayes and Harlington. He was a rather quiet sort of chap, he didn't push himself, but he was promoted to be progress manager there in one of their places and it was too much for him, he found that he had to retire. He was in the Air Force in both wars, and he'd been wounded too."

Frithjof's worst injuries were the result of a freak accident on the airfield where he was working during the Second World War. A plane came in, out of control, hitting the one that Frithjof and two other men were working on. The others were killed, and 'Fritters' was tossed up into the air and impaled on spiked railings nearby. Although he survived this horrifying accident, his health was always affected by it, and he died in Ipswich in 1971.

Comparisons - Piers Ghyll from Gable by Alfred (above) and by William (below). Simultaneous working, 1923

William followed in Alfred's footsteps to become an art student in London, returning to Ambleside only during holidays, and Una was the only one of the four left still living at home.

Mathilde's arthritis worsened, but in spite of her lameness, she still managed to make the daily walk very slowly and painfully from Compston Road to the studio at the top of Wansfell Road, where she would sit in a chair all day, hardly getting up at all. It had been some years since she had been able to go on family outings, unless she could be taken in her wheelchair, and Alfred travelled everywhere on his own to produce the travel guide commissions which continued to trickle from Blacks, about once a year.

Once the war was over, foreign travel was possible again. English visitors wished to take foreign holidays in increasing numbers, and to answer this demand, Alfred was sent abroad to paint several times during the next few years.

Old Fell Gate, Esthwaite

A·HEATON·COOPER

Zermatt, 1921

Chapter Six

Travels

1920-1926

Throughout the 1920s, A & C Black brought Alfred a steady stream of commissions for new books about places both at home and abroad in Europe. Anyone who admires Alfred's work has to admit that the paintings he produced for these books were often not among his best. Not only was he limited by what the commission itself demanded, which often involved painting a familiar landmark from its most famous view point rather than the one Alfred might have preferred; but he was also restricted by the limitations of colour printing and the simplicity and clarity of style required to make poor quality reproductions look as good as possible. So, in time, Alfred developed techniques for illustrations which, when compared with his ordinary studio exhibition paintings, looked rather dull. The illustrations lack the sheer joy and excitement in nature that shine from the heart of Alfred's brightest and best landscape work.

In addition to the strictures of colour re-production, Alfred also had a string of different writers to work with, whose prose he had to illustrate. Their styles were as varied as their opinions; for example, contrast the 1922 edition of MacKenzie MacBride's *Wild Lakeland* with the 1925 edition of W T Palmer's classic, *The English Lakes*. Both books were illustrated by Alfred, but had very different things to say, for instance, about Grasmere:

"Grasmere is well known as a climbing centre, but it is more than that," writes MacBride. *"It is, of all the Lake District villages, the richest in gardens and flowers. The magnificent gardens of Lake Road, Windermere, are show places and from them we can get one of the finest views of the splendid Crinkle Crags and Bowfell group, but Grasmere is a homely spot and she wears her flowers naturally as the May Queen's garland are worn by a country maid. Grasmere charms you with its simplicity as well as by its beauty. The village - we can call Grasmere a village without offending the villager - is also more local than modernised Windermere and ambitious Ambleside."*

But Grasmere's homely garlands failed to charm Palmer:

"Grasmere is in itself without especial charm to the visitor," he wrote in the 1925 edition of his book, again illustrated by Alfred. *"It is too busy to grow beautiful; romance has stayed away, commercialism reigns and I for one do not care a fig for the place outside its connection with the poet, with its great possession, his grave and grey-towered church. But Grasmere as a centre for rambles is unparalleled,"* he conceded.

However difficult Alfred found it to make his paintings all things to all men, at least the book commissions gave him the freedom to paint at will the

The Bield, Little Langdale

rest of the year, even when his prolific output outnumbered sales. He had a steady income, however small; Blacks sent him to Norfolk and Suffolk, County Durham, Somerset and Derbyshire, adventures which he undoubtedly enjoyed. William accompanied him on one or two occasions, and even produced paintings for the commission.

Alfred's preliminary sketches were becoming ever scantier. All that he needed to complete a painting back at his studio was the roughest of outlines, the briefest of notes on colour and his memory and experience did the rest. It was clearly a departure from his youthful ideal of starting and completing each picture out of doors, on the spot, in one session. But the requirements of book illustration were not to capture the mood of Nature at one particular moment of creation. Alfred's brief was simply to produce a picture of some much-loved beauty spot which encapsulated within it all the most familiar features that readers would recognise with affection. It was unimportant to Blacks that a momentary shaft of light on a particular day might mellow the ancient stones of the bridge or church tower he was painting in a way that Alfred would have wanted to capture forever; more important that the reader should recognise the famous bridge and church tower, whatever the mood or light that day. Creating an impression in the *plein air* tradition had little part to play in producing ilustrations for Blacks *"Beautiful Britain"* volumes or *"Twenty Shilling Series"*.

In 1924 Alfred, Mathilde, Una and Aunt Otalia moved to Cross Brow, a sizeable but damp house situated in a hollow along Old Lake Road in Ambleside. The house had belonged to the poet, Sir William Watson, little known now but most popular in his time. It was Alfred's last move, and an

Eiger and Monch, dawn, 1921

important one. Not only was the house famous because of its previous occupant, but it also represented success and stability in Alfred's career, and having been the 'poet's house' it soon became 'Mr Heaton Cooper, the Artist's house.'

The origins of its name had prompted William Watson to write a poem relating the history of the house. Alfred kept a copy of it among his documents, and a framed version of it still hangs on the wall at Cross Brow:

My smallest daughter had wondered how
Her dear home came by its name, Cross Brow:
Her house 'mid the meres, that loveliest seem
In their autumn trance and their winter dream:
Her home at the foot of the mountains high
That have entanglement in the sky.

So I told her how, in a time half known,
And half forgotten, a Cross of stone,
Betwixt field and fellside, here had stood,
More frail than a certain Cross of Wood;
And how sweet souls that fared this way
May have halted before it to kneel and pray.
It is seen no longer, from dale or hill,

'Tis the Cross of Wood that is lasting still!
But here, in a world of pain and loss,
Where each must carry his destined cross,
A frolicsome child remembers now
Why the house she romps in is called Cross Brow,
Though little indeed Life's gleeful morn,
Can know of the Brow that was crowned with thorn.

Perhaps Sir William Watson's poem inspired the new occupants to write again about the house; another poem, called simply *To Cross Brow* was also kept among Alfred's papers. The poem is anonymous, the hand writing elderly and a little shaky, unlike Alfred's firm script. Mathilde and Otalia, who never really managed to come to grips with the complexities of the English language, let alone its poetry, would hardly have been the writers. But whoever it was not only loved the old house, but the people who lived in it and the flowers that grew in the garden, too:

Matterhorn from near Zermatt, 1921

> *Dear Cross Brow! 'neath your sheltering eaves*
> *Beat honest hearts and true;*
> *No cross brows there! for love supreme*
> *Beams from their eyes - and you.*
>
> *And O, your garden of delight,*
> *With flowering borders set,*
> *Of Pinks and Thyme, and Marjoram,*
> *And fragrant Mignonette.*
>
> *Of 'Painted Ladies', jocund, gay,*
> *In serried ranks between;*
> *Attendants on the Rose of Love,*
> *Their well-beloved Queen.*
>
> *There Rosemary and Pansies speak,*
> *With eloquence of past years;*
> *Remembrance Sweet, and thoughts that lie*
> *Full-oft too deep for tears.*
>
> *Dear friends, upon my heart I'll place*
> *Of these a fadeless knot.*
> *And may I add one tiny flower?*
> *The blue Forget me not.*

Quite why Cross Brow should have inspired such flowery and romantic verses is not clear. The garden may well have been the very epitome of English loveliness, but the house inside was not. Extensive alterations and building work have banished these problems today, but when Alfred and Mathilde lived there, it only took a moderate rainfall before the stream opposite the house, which tumbled down from the slopes of Wansfell above, became a small torrent, causing the walls of the damp house in the hollow to run with moisture.

The world at large, or at least society in Ambleside saw the family's move to Cross Brow as the peak of Alfred's success; but the daily struggle to maintain this "success", and keep the family warm, dry and fed was as hard for Alfred as it had ever been.

Alfred could never miss an opportunity of encouraging a sale. He sometimes made opportunist presentations, such as he did in the summer of 1924, just after the family had moved to Cross Brow. Realising the numbers of American and European visitors who called in at the Charing Cross headquarters of The English Speaking Union, he tried to present the E.S.U. with a painting of Grasmere Church. But this was against the rules. Fortunately his bridge partner and former neighbour, Sir George McKay, was a member of the E.S.U. and was able to present the gift as though coming from himself. Alfred's interest in the E.S.U. was minimal but his interest in American patronage rather stronger. Here is the letter of thanks he received which was typical of many others:

Sept 29th 1924

Dear Sir,

Many thanks for your letter of the 17th. It was an inexcusable oversight on our part not to have written sooner to acknowledge your generous gift to the English-Speaking Union of the painting of Grasmere Church, which occupies one of the most prominent positions in our rooms.

The formal presentation was made just before the holiday season, and amidst the almost overwhelming rush of overseas visitors we have had all the summer, the duty of writing to you escaped my memory. The picture is inscribed as a gift from Sir George Mills McKay because, as I understand he explained to you, it was not possible to establish a precedent by accepting the gift of a picture direct from an artist. We are deeply sensible of your generous and practical interest in the English-Speaking Union, and I am sure that one result at least of the gift of "Grasmere Church" will be an increased demand for your work among the many American visitors to the E.S.U. rooms who have remarked on the charm of the picture.

Believe me,
Yours very truly,
Alfred C. Thomas
Executive Secretary.

The struggle to stay one step ahead of the housekeeping bills continued throughout 1925; it must, therefore, have come as a welcome break when Blacks commissioned Alfred to visit Sweden, Lappland and Denmark in 1926, to produce illustrations for two new books. *Sweden* by Dudley Heathcote in their *"Popular and New"* series was published in 1927, and *Denmark*, by Clive Holland, in 1928.

Alfred was accustomed to travelling alone but having such a friendly and inquiring nature he was never very long without a companion.

It is likely that a man like Alfred kept a diary whenever he made journeys of special interest. When he travelled for Blacks, it was important to note down the details of his travel and accommodation, and somebody with such lively powers of observation would have found it difficult not to jot down the odd impression or two as his adventures unfolded. Fortunately, part of Alfred's 1926 travel diary has been kept; unfortunately, most of it is missing, and there are no other known diaries still in existence.

This is hardly surprising, considering the way in which Alfred kept his Swedish diary. Anyone tidying out his drawers would have been forgiven for thinking these torn up scraps of rough paper covered in cramped writing which formed the diary were nothing more than old shopping lists. Paper seemed such a scarce commodity that Alfred's pencilled entries cover every inch of each page, and when he reached the bottom of the page, he would continue by filling the margin too.

The result is chaos. Fortunately Alfred numbered the scraps of paper in the order that they should be read, though he was forced to resort to subdivisions like pages 2 and 2a. Only the most curious of readers would attempt to decipher the maze, which required a magnifying glass to unravel. Perhaps Alfred

Fredericksborg Castle, Copenhagen, 1926

The Rock of Cashel, Co. Tipperary, 1915

Whitby Abbey, 1921

Herring curing houses, East Cliff, Whitby, 1921

Staithes (after the boats come in), 1921

intended to copy his notes out neatly one day; if this was the way in which he always kept his travel journal, his rough notes will almost certainly have been destroyed, quite understandably, and it is by sheer accident that the Swedish diary has survived, at least in part.

This diary is not merely a travelogue of Sweden in the 1920s or the meanderings of an English artist as he painted at will among the lakes and birches of Scandinavia. Alfred had far more to consider than mere scenery. He had introductions to acquire and follow up. There were free train and boat tickets to secure, there were consuls and attachés, minor royalty and wealthy patrons to impress, not only with his paintings but with the idea of a book which would encourage English tourists to visit Sweden, Lappland and Denmark.

His publishers expected him to act as their ambassador, sales representative and English landscape artist of renown while staying in the cheapest of *pensions* and relying on whatever hospitality he was offered, including the use, wherever possible, of free transport.

Fortunately, Alfred's genial nature and pleasant, though slightly artistic appearance appealed to the wealthy and cultured. He was a simple,

Figures at Whitby Market, 1921

uncomplicated man who was visibly impressed by position and class, and he was uncritical of his hosts and pleased to receive their attentions. He told people the things they wanted to hear, and he never made anybody feel uncomfortable by arguing a point, or taking up a moral stand. He was an easy guest, never troublesome or demanding, and he was well-liked wherever he went.

The extract from Alfred's diary covers only the first few weeks in Sweden of a trip which lasted for three months. But even such a short section speaks of the vital importance of patronage and it also shows Alfred as both painter and self-employed businessman, who had to account for every penny he spent. He loved amusing company, good hearty food and a cigar after dinner; few of his wealthy patrons, amused to see the artist munching a lunchtime bread roll while he continued to paint, would have guessed that the bread had been carefully removed from yesterday's breakfast table and preserved in Alfred's useful and accommodating pockets!

These are the brief impressions which he scribbled over the rough, torn pages of a very cheap notebook:

DIARY OF VISIT TO SWEDEN
May/June 1926.

Arrived at Tilbury (with Heaton) and boarded SS Patricia on Sat 22 May. Weather splendid, sea like a lake, came on drizzle towards evening. (Aston Villa footballers on steamer...) excellent food on board of a type one is accustomed to in Norway which is very delightful.

On Sunday interviewed Captain Korvist on board - a fine old sea dog- arrived at Göteborg at 8.30a.m. After Customs exam. I stayed on the upper deck of Patricia and sketched the harbour in shelter from the rain - was advised to stay at The Grand Hotel, Hagenband by a Mr A. Janssen by telefon - he's the manager of the Göta Canal Co. and I am to interview him tomorrow (Tuesday) at 10a.m. as to the travelling passes on the canal to Stockholm etc.

Awful rain all the time on Monday and being Whit Monday all shops closed and drenching rain prevailed all day and evening which gave one a rather bad impression of this town of Kondsomer, hotels and shops. Met the British Consul on board at Gothenburg and he invited me to call on him in Göteborg before leaving.

Tuesday May 25th, called on Mr Jonnsen at the Göta Kanal offices at 10.a.m. and he gave me a free pass from Jönköping to Stockholm. He was very much interested in the project for the book and said it would do Sweden a lot of good - He also gave me a letter of introduction to Herr Hammfoged E. Guldstrom at Vadstena on Lake Vättern.

At "Are Fresk's Pensionnat". "Nils Tommason", Photographer and car owner for Tannefors. 2.15 from Göteborg. Tuesday. Steamer to Marstrand (stay night) Marstrand to Lysekil. About 10a.m. arriving 2p.m. Wednesday. Leave Lysekil at 4.35p.m. for Trollhättän. Called on A. Jannsen and received from him free ticket on Göta Kanal and free meals on board - also on their steamer down L. Vättern to Jönköping and from there by rail to Stockholm and Mr Johnson has made it known to all concerned on the route so that I shall be well looked after. At Vadstena - deliver letter of introduction to Herr Hammmersfog de Guldstrom (Captain Class Grill, Göta Canal s/s Gothenburg), along with Herr A. Jonnsen at the Göta Kanal offices at Gothenburg. Lunched with him at the Botanical Gardens Restaurant on Tuesday and he took me to the steamer for Marstrand after lunch. He telephoned for free ticket for the journey from Lysekil to Trollhättän, which I shall have handed to me at Lysekil on Wednesday 26th May (which was not granted). Arrived at Trollhättän and sketched the falls - stayed at a very cheap apartment house, very clean.

Thursday - Joined the Göta Kanal steamer "Ceres" at 5 pm. on Friday 28th May in brilliant weather. At 2 am. we arrive at Sjötorp where there are a number of locks and as we have sailed up to that time on Lake Vänern it is quite refreshing to come to land again if only for a short time. It is quite light

Vadstena Castle, Sweden, 1926

Jönköping, 1926

at 2 am. and I get sketches from the steamer of several places on that part of the Canal. We steamed through several lakes very much like Windermere but very much larger. The country is very flat, with large forests of firs and Birch trees and many wooded islands on this immense lake - like a sea, there being no land in sight down the lake.

Arrived at Vadstena at 3p.m. and was introduced to Herr Hammfoged E Guldstrom by the Captain of the Ceres - I gave him Mr Jonnsen's letter and he very kindly asked me to have a chat with him at 5 at the Hotel at Vadstena. He insisted on being my host and would not allow me to pay for the coffee and so we spent a very pleasant evening. This was Saturday May 29th.

On Sunday morning I painted a picture of Vadstena Castle and in the afternoon Herr Guldstrom called at the Hotel at 3 and took me round the old town and in the castle. Also St Bridget's home and Convent, the ancient church and finally to his home. He is an old bachelor (72) but a fine type of man - tall and good looking - rather fat under the waist. He has a very charming house, bright and roomy and a lot of curios and old furniture belonged to his parents. He also showed me the grave in which his parents rest (quite pathetic). He insisted on my having dinner with him at the hotel and gave me a most enjoyable dinner of about six courses, and it was accompanied with several wines - we adjourned to the smoking room and had coffee and cigars until 11 pm. when we retired. I saw him on Monday morning 12.30p.m. on joining the steamer for Jönköping, noted for tandstickoe, and said farewell to the jolly old man - arrived at Jönköping at 9p.m. and on the following morning made a picture of the town. The weather (2 kronen 25 ore sounds like tyngefern) was drizzly but I got a decent sketch from the Stads Park high over the town. Sheltered by the trees. At 3.53p.m. I got the train to Linköping arriving shortly after 9p.m. Outdoor restaurants and bands in ornamental grounds lit up with coloured electric lamps and among the trees looked quite attractive. Very good selections of music produced by a quartet - piano, 2 violins and a large fiddle which was on the ground, I forget its name. As one must always have refreshments with food it is sometimes inconvenient. Could not find anything to paint at Linköping so went on to Stockholm arriving at about 6p.m. after a long and rather tedious journey through flat country, cultivated in parts but mostly fir and birch forests, between the stops at the smaller stations.

Wednesday 2nd June - stayed at the Park Hotel. I must sleep in a bed let into the wall. For breakfast I had oatmeal porridge and two boiled eggs - and for lunch a couple of sandwiches of cheese which I had pinched from a former meal several days ago. I had to soak with water and the bread had gone hard.

In the morning 3rd June Thursday I called at 10.a.m. on Commander Peyron as I was asked to do by Mr Erik Carlsten of London. (Swedish Travel Bureau) I found him a most agreeable man and anxious to do all he can for me. Got a friend to motor me round Stockholm City on the same morning and another friend of his Colonel Poignant to motor me round the outskirts in the aft. Commander Peyron also wishes me to meet Prince Eugen and will arrange it tomorrow (Friday). He has also arranged for me to visit some *very rich friends of his a few miles out of Stockholm who will send their motor for me on Sunday morning and I am to spend the day there with them and take my sketching things. (Their motor calls at 10a.m.)*

City Hall,Stockholm, 1926

Stockholm - Mrs Leppar of Central Station Bureau took me round the city (Town Hall from a small street over on quay) Colonel Poignant calls at Hotel Park at 3 pm. to take me round to see Stockholm's environment. From what I have seen of Stockholm I will paint one picture of the Royal Palace from the Opera House. Also a picture of the new Town Hall from the quayside. Also the old Hansa Quay and open air, market stalls and shipping.

On Thursday evening, June 3rd, dined at Den Gyldene Freden in the old cellars by candle and lamp light. (Commander Peyron told me of it, a 14th century house given by the painter Andreas Tom to the city a few years ago and kept in that quaint old style - simple and darkish, a series of thick walled vaulted cellars - on different levels furnished with simple oak tables and mats on the tables (no table cloth). A lively company of townsfolk, etc. eating and smoking by the weird light and dusky shades. The candlesticks similar to ours at home (The petticoat puttom in brass) ancient lamps in different quaint shapes hang on the walls which show the roughness of the old bricks and stone.

For dinner I had
Sour Milk (curded, thick)
Fish
Duck (roast)
Rhubarb
(and Dark Beer)
a cup of coffee.   All for 3Kr 50

Friday June 4th Call at the office of Commander Peyron at 9.45a.m. He telephoned to HRH Prince Eugen and got an appointment for us to see him at 12.30p.m. Painted from 10 to 3 on the City Hall and from 3.15 to 4.45p.m. on the Palace and water (from Opera House cafe balcony) also from 5.15 to 7.15p.m. glorious sunshine but had to leave it to meet the train to Djursholm station to a place named Germania. Comm. Peyron meets the train at Bragevagen (noisy motor cars and aeroplanes all day long - - -) and we go to see some friends of his and a good view.

Send from publishers books to the following: HRH Prince Eugen, Stockholm; Herr Jonnsen, Gothenborg; Commander Peyron, Stockholm; Mrs Hammfoged, Vadstena... and a sketch of Lakeland on arr. home to H.R.H. Prince Eugen. Admiral Peyron.

Saturday 5th June at 11a.m. Went with Comm Peyron to the house of HRH Prince Eugen and was received very gracefully by him, had an hour's chat on Art etc. and he was very interested in the book on Sweden I am doing. Also he suggested a place or 2 on the South West Coast, Kullen Rocks and Bästad as being picturesque. H.R.H. has a fine Art Gallery of modern Swedish art as well as some pictures of his own there. The view across Lake Malaren is fine from his terrace garden.

*Harsprånget Falls,
Gripsholm, 1926*

Sunday 6th June spent all day with some friends of Peyron who called for me in their car. We went miles along lakes and stretches of the Baltic with interminable woods of larch pine and birch. Picnicked by the Lake Malaren under the trees - very hot day. Mr Odelbery, Mrs O and Miss O and myself - also a big French Poodle. Drove home to their house and had a glorious dinner and wines, cigars and coffee - and they sent me back by motor in the evening. Mr Odleberg owns a large chinaware factory near their house and they produce some glorious lustre and other ware. Also owns a fleet of steamers. They want me to go again to see through the works on my return to Stockholm but I cannot go as my time is everything for the book.

Monday 7th June Went by train to Gripsholm to paint the Royal castle there, it is quite a distance from Stockholm (perhaps 28 miles). Had food at Gyldene Freden and got back to hotel about 9.30p.m.

Tuesday 8th June saw Peyron in morning and got from him all the free tickets for the journey through Sweden and from another man free tickets for the motor launches on the Lapland Lakes. Left Stockholm at 1 o'clock for Uppsala where I painted Gamle Upsala - the Kings Tombs, mounds from the 6th century.

Wednesday June 9th Came to Leksand on the Siljan lakes and stayed the night - nothing there to paint so went to Rättvik, a most beautiful and paintable place. Was introduced by Peyron to a lady (by letter) and she has a wonderfully fine pensionnat where I got room and food for 8.50 per day (very cheap for Sweden) The pensionnat is in beautiful woods of birch with glimpses of the lake and the fine old church. I am making a picture of the peasants in their costumes going to church in long boats. And as I shall be here on Sunday I shall see quite a bright gathering if fine. Miss Hilda Renstrom is the hostess at the pensionnat. She has 3 houses, one a large one all in the woods and near to each other and built in the old Swedish style. She took me along with a friend of hers to see a professor architect who lives near in a charming old world house and we strolled through the gardens and into the house - which is kept in the old style throughout - The old 'pris' and old china and furniture - some rose malet - quite a charming old man and his wife. He lives in Stockholm in the winter. Has painted a few things in watercolour.

On Friday 11th I went to Mora and painted the church and fine old bell tower which stands apart from the church - a fine picture. Walked down to Rättvik church in the evening and made a study.

Saturday the 12th. I painted Rättvik Church...

The diary continues and indicates that he travelled north to Abisko in Lappland, then to Lulea on the Gulf of Bothnia, and at the beginning of July he was in Gotland, Oland and eventually Copenhagen, returning home after a further two weeks.

The sketches that he made abroad on his travels are very different from his Lakeland outlines. Aware that he was on unfamiliar territory and that he would have only the one chance to view the scene before continuing his

Abisko, Lake Torneträsk, 1926

journey, Alfred started to use larger sketch books, with bigger pages, and he filled these with detailed drawings, which he then painted in with watercolours. He left very little to memory while painting in Sweden and Denmark, preferring instead to produce as the working sketch a swift, miniature version of the painting which would evolve. His habit at home was quite the reverse; a few rough lines, and a note or two on the time and the light was all he needed to produce a Lakeland landscape.

These preliminary water colours that Alfred began producing were as valuable a guide as a colour photograph used by an artist today. Finding it easier than trusting to memory when away from the landscape he knew so well, Alfred continued to use this method when he went to North Wales that same autumn to produce yet more illustration for another Blacks book.

Here is his own report of the Sweden/Denmark trip which he wrote for A & C Black:

Augt, '26

Messrs A and C Black,

Sweden and Denmark.

Having returned from these countries I have pleasure in enclosing you lists of the pictures for the coming volumes on these two countries. The pictures are in active preparation and I hope to be able to deliver Sweden to you by the end of October.

Sweden: Commander Peyron, Head of the Swedish Tourist Bureau in Stockholm (12 Vasgatan) arranged everything to facilitate my travelling throughout Sweden and gave me an open letter to all local branches of the Bureau at nearly all the places I visited. (I looked them all up and explained to them the nature of my business.) Com. Peyron handed to me free travelling passes on all the State Railways and Dr Anvik, Head of the - granted me free travel on all their motorboats on the Lappland lakes, and I was a free guest at their tourist stations.

Lapplander, 1926

A café at Porjus, 1926

At Stockholm I was introduced by Admiral Peyron to His Royal Highness Prince Eugen at his residence near Stockholm, and as the Prince is a well-known artist himself, he was intensely interested in the book on Sweden and suggested one or two of the pictures. I found the Swedish people everywhere most kind and hospitable.

The Gotha Canal Company gave me a free pass on the Canal, through the kindness of Her Johnson, the Manager at Gothenburg, who saw in the forthcoming book great propaganda for Sweden.

Lappland is most attractive to the tourist and new routes are opening out on the Great Lakes there this year right through to Narvik in northern Norway. The Siljan lakes, in Dalcalia, are beautiful and the peasants still wear the bright national costume. I showed pictures of the places where the great industries in timber and iron are found, and have been complimented by the high authorities on the selection of places represented on the list.

Denmark: At Copenhagen I was handed free travelling tickets through Denmark by Her Udenrigsmunstan Paulsen at Christiansborg Castle so I was enabled to get freely about and was treated by everyone concerned with the greatest kindness. Her Moller-Holst, Head of the Tourist Bureau for Denmark, gave me an open letter of introduction to all branches of the Tourist Bureau throughout Denmark - which came in very useful - and I used them as propaganda for the book.

I was fortunate in the weather in both countries and was able to get some bright and attractive pictures of the chief places of interest to tourists and others. I write all this at the risk of boring you with so much detail.

With kind regards,
Yours Faithfully,
A.H.C.

In his customary way, Alfred thanked those who had smoothed his path through Sweden and Denmark with gifts of paintings and copies of his books, sent through the post from Ambleside. Many of those who wrote to thank Alfred asked to be told when the books about Sweden and Denmark would be published, so that they could purchase copies to give away to family and friends. Others told him they had bought originals from Fritze Bokhandel in Stockholm. Another dealer, with whom Alfred left about 30 watercolours, managed to sell a job lot of 23 paintings to a shipping line, to be exhibited on one of their passenger ships. Alfred was delighted to accept 3,000 Kr. in payment for the deal. A & C Black even allowed Alfred to permit another shipping line the right to reproduce two other paintings, "if it would help you to effect sales", provided that the rights were limited to Sweden and must not interfere in any way with the circulation of the book in that country.

Such deals with companies like shipping lines were of far greater benefit than the patronage of individuals such as Royalty. The audience that Alfred had cleverly landed with the Royal artist, Prince Eugen, reported by Alfred to be "intensely" interested in his work, yielded nothing more than a brief, courtesy note in return for one of Alfred's Lakeland books, which he sent as a gift:

Dear Mr Heaton Cooper!

It was very kind of you to remember me with your beautiful book, which gives me the most charming impression of this part of England. I was very pleased to hear that my informations were of some use for your work on Sweden. I will very much enjoy to see the reproductions of your pictures, which I am sure will represent our country in the most favourable light.

Yours sincerely,
Eugen

These "thank you" letters were carefully preserved, either by Alfred or Mathilde. Disappointingly, few other letters were kept, though important signatures were. These signatures, ripped off the end of the letter, were apparently more important to the finder than the actual correspondence, which was discarded. Both Henry Moore and Clausen appear to have written letters to Alfred, but only their signatures remain. Whatever they wrote to Alfred was judged to have been too dull and unimportant to preserve.

Gribscoven, the Kings Pavilion Lake, 1926

Seatoller, foot of Honister Pass

Chapter Seven

Cross Brow

1926-1929

Returning from his travels probably made Alfred even more aware that Cross Brow was in fact a cross to bear, which was becoming heavier with each passing year. Instead of renting the house, as he had rented homes in the past, he had a mortgage to pay; and in addition, there were three dependents, a student son and a maid all relying on Alfred to pay the bills.

Mathilde ventured out very little from the house, unless it was to sit in the studio. She was virtually crippled by now with arthritis and had to be taken everywhere in a bath chair. In the spring of 1927, she went into hospital in Lancaster where there was a noted specialist who treated patients with severe arthritis. Alfred and William wandered up and down the banks of the Lancaster Canal when they went to visit her, and painted canal scapes. Although Mathilde's condition never improved dramatically, she not only outlived Alfred by nearly 30 years, but lived long enough to be Grasmere's oldest resident, dying at the age of ninety.

Aunt Otalia no longer lived with the family. She had a room in Ambleside, but she came in every day to Cross Brow as Mathilde's constant companion, and to help in the house and to do the shopping. Una, who was eighteen, had left the PNEU (Parents' National Educational Union) school at Fairfield; both Una and Ellide had attended this School, which was the first of its kind, run on experimental lines with Charlotte Mason College of Education.

Una loved life, and showed little inclination to do anything at all except play tennis, rock climb and have fun. She disliked helping in the house and was unwilling to help at all in her father's studio. She was the only one of the four children left at home except when William, who was at Art College in London, came home for holidays.

The family's maid was Molly Strickland, who still lives in Ambleside. She slept in a tiny bedroom next to the bathroom, and was paid seven shillings and sixpence a week, which wasn't very much, even in those days. But she became very fond of all the family, and remained loyal to Mathilde for several years.

Even the closest of families occasionally quarrel. However harmonious their relationships appear to the outside world, home is the place where families can express their tensions and frustrations. It would be very unusual to live with a family and never hear a raised voice, especially from the head

Alfred at the Log House Studio, 1927

of the household. But Alfred was unusual. He was never angry, being always and at all times the perfect gentleman:

"He was a peaceful sort of man, I never heard him fall out or anything like that - and, I mean, when you live in a place you do hear them shouting at one another. But he never did, never. He was what he was - a gentleman. His work was his life, he didn't want anything else", Molly recalled.

One day, Molly had an accident as she cleaned the studio:

"My mother-in-law came down to help me clean this room, and she spilled some stuff on one of his paintings on the wall. It was an expensive one, and I had to tell him, because I was so bothered about it. 'My dear', he said - and I can always remember his face, 'My dear, don't you worry. I'll soon have that sorted out.' And he did. I think he must have painted over the stain."

Molly loved browsing through the paintings as she cleaned:

"He was a wonderful painter. I've never seen any painted that I liked as much as I liked his. Even though I was only working, I used to go down there and clean the Log Cabin and I used to go round and have a look at them all. They all had prices on them, ready for being sold. I think if I'd asked him to paint one for me, I think he would have done. I loved working for them."

The Log House Studio (bottom left), 1930's

Whatever Ambleside society imagined about life with the

Artist at Cross Brow, Molly saw the reality at close quarters. She was the same age as Una - yet it was her lot in life to scrub the bare flags on the kitchen floor while Una sat and watched. Young as she was, Molly developed a painful housemaid's knee:

"Her mother told Una to get down and do the kitchen floor, because you used to have to get down on your hands and knees then, there was no mops and things. And she was supposed to have done it. Her mother thought she had done it and she hadn't. She used to skive off behind her mother!"

Molly knew enough about poverty to recognise it in the Heaton Cooper household. What she witnessed made her feel very sympathetic to the family's difficulties:

"They were poor, though, in those days. They really were. They hadn't anything. I used to give them recipes my mother had because they were cheap - they were so poor.

"... I used to get up in the morning and make the breakfast and they never had a big breakfast, bacon and eggs, because they couldn't afford it. Every week Auntie (Otalia) used to get half a pound of butter and half a pound of margerine and they were mixed together. She couldn't afford butter on its own, and we had to have that and cut it up in pieces and put it on the table. Oh, they did live like poor mice, they really did. They couldn't afford anything. They had to sell a picture to buy anything, you see. And Una wasn't any help. She never worked. She was a bonny lass and I used to get her out of all these scrapes, chasing her, fetching her home. And she used to say to me, 'Molly, I'm going to be an old man's darling, not a young man's slave.' And she was. She married old Mr Lee, and he was white-haired then!"

Life at Cross Brow was austere. The floorboards were bare and uncarpeted, with only a few rugs to cover them. The kitchen and scullery were furnished with just an old wooden table and a larder cupboard, where Otalia's Norwegian pickled beef was stored. Otalia did most of the cooking and controlled the purse strings in the kitchen, making sure nobody had more than their share. Molly did the washing in the back scullery in a dolly tub, and everybody wore thick underwear to keep out the cold and damp.

Maid with eggs

Alfred spent most of his time out on the fells, painting. He would leave after breakfast, wearing his tweed suit with knickerbockers and a tweed hat; but the trousers and the jacket no longer matched exactly, though Alfred never looked anything but neatly dressed despite the age of his clothes. Molly often made him a picnic lunch to take with him - usually it was something cheap and filling like thick jam sandwiches.

He painted in all weathers, and never stayed all day in the house however cold and wet it was outside. It was his custom every evening to return home via the *Royal Oak*, a very old public house at the top of Church Street in Ambleside. He would call in on his way home to meet his friends, many of them huntsmen and farmers who had been out on the fells all day too. Alfred

Great Gable and Sprinkling Tarn

never drank more than a half pint of beer, but sometimes he would vary his routine and call instead at the Conservative Club nearby for a game of billiards, which he enjoyed immensely.

It was also his pleasure to call in at one of the grocery shops to buy some very small delicacy that the family could share. It might be little more than a bowl of whelks or cockles, but he bought whatever he could afford. He was punctual, arriving home before the evening meal, never later than about half past six, and Mathilde made sure each cold evening that the fire in the sitting room was banked up and blazing to warm him on his return.

Dinner was always eaten in the dining room with the table correctly set and a table cloth, glasses and water jug.

"They knew how to live, but they didn't have the money to keep it up... Alfred used to come back at teatime but he never went out again after he had his dinner - well, it was more like a tea, really, because we didn't have much. I always remember my Dad used to have two slices of bread and butter and I used to put it in a pan of milk, and grate cheese and salt and pepper and then pour it over this bread. Well, I made it for them one night, but I did it on toast, not just bread. Alfred was over the moon! He told us to put it in a soup tureen because it was all sloppy, and he did enjoy it. He really did! 'My', he said, 'That was good Molly!' On Monday dinnertime they always had cold meat from the joint on Sunday and macaroni cheese. I used to hate it!"

Each year Alfred faced a rent increase for the land on which he had built the studio. He felt that the cost of leasing the land, at the top of Wansfell Road, had increased so unfairly, that he decided to move again. He purchased a small piece of land at Fisherbeck on the main approach road into the village, and in 1928 he moved the studio once again, re-assembling it as before.

Social life at Cross Brow was very quiet, now only Una was left at home. Alfred very rarely went out in the evening, and Mathilde never did. The family had no wireless, and no daily paper; there were few books in the house. After dinner in the evening, Molly would sit in the kitchen while the family sat quietly in the sittingroom. Very occasionally, friends might call round for an evening of bridge. Sir George and Lady McKay were among the most frequent social visitors.

Neither Alfred nor Mathilde were good letter writers. In the absence of regular correspondence with Alfred's brothers and sister, Edith, the family lost touch with each other for years at a time, and the only occasion for a letter to be written was when something specific had to be discussed.

Alfred and Mathilde and the children had visited Edith and her journalist husband, Jean Gautreau, before the first World War, but since that time the only occasion for an exchange of news was when Mathilde wrote asking if Gautreau could find Frithjof a job in the St. Nazaire shipyards, where Gautreau represented his paper, *L'Echo de la Loire*. Due to the political

Pillar from Scarth Gap, 1910

situation at the time, Gautreau was unable to help, but he regretted this very much. Finally, he wrote to Alfred in April 1927, asking for news of the family. But with no mention whatsoever of his wife, Edith, it would appear that Alfred's sister had died sometime before:

Dear Brother,

I often think of you and of old England and wonder what is becoming of you all.

I just came across a letter from Sister Mathilde containing a few words, and even verses from little Frithjof. I was very sorry not being able to do anything for him here at the time you wrote to me. I would have been very pleased to find him a good job in local yards here. The thing was half-arranged (I am very friendly with the managers) when Lloyd George delivered his attacks on France. That stopped instantly the application for British workmen that I had set going in collaboration with the English Consul. I wanted Frithjof to be taken in as an 'ingenieur': for that English workmen were necessarily wanted in the Yard, as F. does not know French. After Lloyd George's sortie the yards here gave up thinking of English labour.

Just let me know what is becoming of little Frithjof... ("I'll tell policeman!! That is very far back - and we are getting old) and Pretty Boy? and little Ellida? And Una whom I have never seen?

I, many times, have thought I would like to see you all again. Unfortunately travelling is so very expensive with the actual rate of exchange. Still I may go to London in the spring for a Paris journal (articles on England.) If that comes off I will let you know and perhaps we could meet in London... and we have so much to say, each of us.

I have often thought of your coming for a week or so to my house in St. Nazaire and painting round. Are you always working for Blacks? We have here an English painter, Miss T. Harmar, and an English lord (friend of mine) Lord Harberton, a genial old boozer.

I got your portrait in a Lancashire weekly. How are you getting on with your painting? I often look for your name on the list of the R.I. or R.A.

Believe me,
Ever yours affectionately,
With best wishes and kind regards to all,
J.B. Gautreau.

What has become of Dan and family?? A long letter, please

Alfred must have replied at last, because the letter was followed up within a few weeks by a visit from Jean Gautreau to Ambleside. His visit co-incided with Mathilde's stay in hospital in Lancaster. But the thankyou letter that he wrote in August, 1927, is valuable for the description it unwittingly supplies of life at Cross Brow:

My dear Brother,

I am rather late in thanking you for your kind welcome in beautiful Ambleside, of which I preserve a pleasant souvenir. No doubt it is now full of visitors, millionaires, who buy pictures. I wish you all the success your great, ever-growing talent deserves. I wish you also to come to France to paint the beautiful Loire valley. I would do, when you are here, everything in my power to help facilitate your work.

I hope gentle "little" Una is ever the pretty and happy picture of good health. By now sister Mathilde has no doubt regained her home in better health. I see in imagination your comfortable and pleasant "estate" with devoted Otalia looking after the "non-artistic" wants of the inmates.

On leaving Ambleside I went straight to London. I got there invitations to visit the Vickers and Cammel Laird works, Birkenhead. Unfortunately, I had no longer any time left and did not want to go back. I am in correspondence with the courteous managers who supply me with all journalistic information I may desire, and fine photos.

Portsmouth next, where I stayed ten days and made many friends. The reception of the French fleet was magnificent, exceeding in warmth anything that had been expected. The French admiral by whom I was received and lunched was delighted. I found all French officers are pro-British and all English officers pro-French. I saw there an English commodore whom I had had the opportunity of welcoming in St Nazaire in the name of the municipality when a British division came in 1924. Too many invitations and cocktails (it reminded me of our reception by generous Sir and Lady McKay): it was time I left: my French health would not have kept pace with these imbibing performances.

I invited Frithjof and Heaton (William) to come and meet me and was disappointed they could not come. Having engagements every day, I could not find time to go and visit the Sanctuary. I received a letter from F who is anxious for a permanent job. If only he knew French, I would easily find him a good post here as I am on good terms with all dockyard managers. Will try.

> *With kind regards to all,*
> *Yours affectionately,*
> *J.B. Gautreau.*

Jean Gautreau could hardly have visited Ambleside without observing the need for funds, hence his remark about millionaire, picture-buying visitors. His brief appraisal of family life at Cross Brow was remarkably accurate; there was Una, being pretty, happy and healthy while Otalia was devoted, Mathilde was unwell and Alfred was painting. The McKays were still entertaining their guests as they always did, with generous amounts to drink; and William (Heaton) was staying at a community of artists called The Sanctuary, in the south of England, where Frithjof came to visit him, still searching for a permanent job during the Depression.

One of the things about Alfred which appealed to his friends was the lack

"Children of the Mist",
Braemar, 1922

The Joiners Shop
Haws Bank, Coniston, 1900

A H Illingworth at Wetherall, 1922

of snobbishness in his choice of companions. He was somebody who was equally at home with the farmers and huntsmen he met on the fells as he was seated at dinner with Sir George and Lady McKay. Throughout the 1920s, one of A.H.C.'s closest friends was 'A.H.I' - A. Holden Illingworth, wealthy industrialist and owner of Dove Nest, near Skelghyll Woods.

Illingworth was well known for his skill as a fisherman. In fact, he knew so much about it and had such vast experience of fishing the waters of Britain, that his *Reminiscences* covered two volumes, published privately. One of Alfred's favourite haunts was Dove Nest Woods, overlooking Lake Windermere and the panorama of mountains behind; perhaps it was one day as he walked through the woods that he and Illingworth first encountered each other. Illingworth dabbled a little himself and had a great interest in art. Alfred loved painting water - so the combination of fishing and painting brought the two men together for hours at a time on the Rivers Eden or Eamont or Wharfe.

It was while the friends shared a couple of contented days at Wetheral, near Carlisle in March, 1922, that Alfred attempted to sketch the accomplished fisherman at work. The two sat in a little punt, or fished from the banks, and their simple pleasures are recorded in one of Alfred's sketch books. Illingworth asked Alfred to illustrate his two volumes of *Reminiscences,* Alfred agreed; he was thinking of the book on one occasion in Whitby when he went to great pains to paint the rainbow colours of a certain fish while sketching for Blacks. The sketch re-appears as an illustration in one of the Illingworth volumes, but Alfred didn't live long enough to enjoy his friend's published tales of fishing. He died three years before either volume was published.

Although Illingworth attempted to set down his fishing adventures on paper, he always felt that words were inadequate to do complete justice to the complexities of fishing. He then recalled Alfred's own reluctance to abandon his paintbrush in favour of a pen as a means of expressing himself:

"I feel safe in saying that the rod is mightier than the pen", Illingworth wrote in the introduction to Volume Two. *"No man's pen has ever yet described the rod and its use with satisfying completeness. The last word will never be said or written and how sad if it was to be.*

"A somewhat comparable dilemma overtook my artist friend, Heaton-Cooper, who made for me certain delightful sketches which illustrate this book. In one instance he was invited by the publishers of the long series of volumes which his pictures of English landscape have adorned, to write as well as illustrate the books. The resulting description and historical notes were warmly commended and accepted, but my friend tells me he would illustrate ten books rather than write one, such was his 'expense of spirit' in venturing upon a craft which was strange to him."

The book Illingworth referred to was *The Norwegian Fjords*, written nearly twenty years previously - but despite the time which had elasped, Alfred was still busy declaring he would never write another!

Alfred went to Norway for the last time in the summer of 1927, pausing to paint at Bergen, Tromso and the Lofoten Islands. The following year, during 1928, he became ill with cancer of the stomach. His last painting journey was to Snowdonia in the autumn, where, in spite of his illness, he produced watercolours of the Welsh mountains and valleys as fine as anything he had done for Blacks throughout his career.

In the summer of 1929, Alfred had an operation at a nursing home in Victoria Park, Manchester. Mathilde remained at home, managing affairs at the Studio, and even arranging a special exhibition. Alfred wrote to her frequently, seemingly quite unaware of the fact that he was dying, or perhaps wishing to protect her from his inner fears. As always, his primary concern was to earn enough to pay the bills. Here are Alfred's last letters:

Pillar Rock of Ennerdale, 1905

Dungeon Ghyll, Great Langdale, 1905

Sunday morning

(don't quite know date)

Min kja're Hustru,

Nothing fresh to report - the same old routine - the slowness of the time are marked features, otherwise tummy mine seems slowly healing and is not quite so painful. The sun shines through the leaves of the trees in the grounds and the little birds are busy collecting worms. Dr Morley seems satisfied and so there is nothing further to feel anxious about.

I hope you are all flourishing at Cross Brow and are getting a few visitors into the Studio.

I have written Bromley to return as many watercolours as he can for the Exhibition. He has quite a lot. Glad you're having the Studio tea party next week. I should like an invitation.

I hope the tortoise has not run away. But I don't think he can.

With much love to Una, Sheila and most for your dearself, and not forgetting dear old Charlie,

*Yours ever,
AHC*

Bromley's, the Bolton art dealers, carried stocks of Alfred's paintings throughout his life. His illness had interrupted his painting so much, that he must have written to ask Bromley's to supply a few extra paintings for the forthcoming exhibition in Ambleside.

Sheila, Ellide and Harold Carson Parker's only daughter, was sent from India to be educated in England and during the holidays she stayed with her grandparents at Cross Brow. The tortoise that Alfred referred to belonged to Una. Molly Strickland, the maid, recalled the time when the family thought the tortoise had died and used it as a doorstop. The tortoise woke up, and the doorstop walked away!

Alfred's letter on Monday, June 24th, was briefer because he was feeling less energetic than the day before. His pain and fatigue are almost tangible through the tired handwriting:

Min Kja're Hustru,

Thanks for your interesting letter. Hope you get quite a number of callers to the Private Views at Studio.

I have written Harrap today but have no stamps and no money, can you send me ten shillings. I owe the barber and newspaper man.

Mrs Leigh came this afternoon and brought some more lovely roses and delphiniums, also a couple of pears and "The Sphere" newspaper.

I don't know that I have any fresh news. Hope you are all keeping fit at Cross Brow.

Love to you all and most for min kja're hustru,

Yours ever,
(sleepy) Alfred.

Three days later, Alfred felt stronger and his sense of humour had returned:

Min kja're Hustru,

I've nothing fresh to report since last letter, but have been considering if you had any visitors to the Studio yesterday in reply to the "Kind Invitation".

I'm afraid you'd be disappointed - Mrs Leigh would send you some nice cakes and flowers which would arrive in the morning !... Glad tidings!!!

I may be home again in a few days but the arrangements are going to be a little awkward. The Leighs want me to spend a few days with them - to recoup - I should much prefer coming home direct and so would you, as I should come on quicker at home. So I hardly know how they will arrange it. I don't want to offend Mrs Leigh but perhaps we can come to a compromise. It is decidedly awkward.

It will be one day next week. I was up for the first time this morning but only for 10 minutes which was grand.

Later - Mrs Leigh and Dick have just called and I think there will be nothing in the way of my coming home direct some day next week.

Mrs Leigh is looking up the cost of an ambulance but am afraid it will be out of the question.

We shall see later,
Much love to you all, and most for yourself,
Yours ever,
Alfred.

Feeding the Hens,
Lowfold, Ambleside, 1926

How typical of Alfred that he should be worrying more about offending the kind but insistent Mrs Leigh than about his own illness; too much of a gentleman to say a straightforward "No" to her invitation, Alfred had spent nearly all day worrying about how to refuse it.

Two days later, Alfred seemed very much more in control of things:

Min Kja're Hustru,

So glad to get your cheerful note this morning and to see from it that you have had such a successful result of the 2 days of the Private View. It will cheer you up and be a good thing for the future. The Studio would look quite bright with the flowers and tasty with the cakes.

I'm so glad you've been able to pay the Rates and Elec. Light. We can deal with the other things later. The Income Tax can wait, so can Asplin and Gibson.

I am getting up every day now and sitting in the sun (in the room). Mrs Leigh comes in about 4 to 5 and Dick, and generally bring something nice.

Do not bother about Fuller from New Zealand. He will be in London now and I shall hear from him on my return home. In the Studio there is a parcel of un-mounted watercolours and among them I have seen several of Whitby cottages etc.

Hope you have a successful day today again and with much love also to Sheila and the tortoise, Una and Nap but mostly for yourself, dear hustru. Love and best wishes to Charlie, also,

Yours ever,
Alfred.

From this last letter it would appear that Mrs Leigh's flowers and cakes sent by parcel did arrive in time for the Private View Tea Party, and that Mathilde sold sufficient pictures to pay the rates and electricity, though the butcher (Asplin) and the grocer (Gibson) both had to wait.

It is very sad that at the end of Alfred's hard working life, his paintings were still insufficiently valuable to pay the household bills. In this respect, he had much in common with some of the most famous painters, poets and musicians the world has ever known, whose posthumous recognition and success arrived too late to provide them with even the simplest of comforts and luxuries during their own lifetimes.

Alfred died on Sunday, July 21st, 1929, at the age of 66, just three weeks after his return home to Cross Brow.

His funeral took place at St Mary's Parish Church, Ambleside, and was conducted jointly by the vicar of Ambleside, the Revd. R.B. Luard-Selby and the Revd. F. Lewis, headmaster of Kelsick School.

The funeral was important enough to attract the local reporter from the *Westmorland Gazette*. His job was to write down the names of the chief mourners, and the list was duly reported in the following issue which appeared on Friday, July 26th. The names show a wide cross-section of friends and townspeople; the doctor, the local solicitors, an artist or two and some of Alfred's hunting companions. The congregation was not a large one, and neither was the family representation. There were only two family mourners: Frithjof and Una. No mention was made of Mathilde's presence at her husband's funeral, or Otalia, his sister-in-law, or even his grand daughter, Sheila.

Why did Mathilde not attend Alfred's funeral? Was the reporter's list incomplete or incorrect? Could Mathilde, crippled as she was, have been wheeled into the church by Otalia in her bathchair in advance of the other mourners and her presence have been omitted by the reporter?

Alfred's other two children were not present, either. Ellide was in India and William was ill at home. He had been in a Margate hospital being treated for suspected tuberculosis when he heard that his father was dying. He was discharged from hospital and began the journey home, stopping in London *en route*, when he received a telephone call to say that he was too late and Alfred had died. He continued the journey home to Cross Brow, but was too ill to attend the funeral. Perhaps Mathilde and Otalia failed to attend Alfred's funeral because they were nursing William?

The mourners listed included members of the Carson Parker family (Ellide's in-laws); a Mr J B Bolton-Heaton of Holme Park, near Kendal; Miss Marjorie Illingworth, daughter of Alfred's fishing friend, A Holden Illingworth; Mr C Hopley; Sir George and Lady McKay from Rothay

Showers over Garburn Pass, 1927

Manor; Mr T Ashworth (Windermere, late of Markland Hill, Bolton); Cuthbert Rigby, the painter and member of the Lake Artists Society; Mrs J A Jackson, a great personal friend of Alfred and Mathilde's; R Logan, representing Alfred's hunting friends; Mr J Scott; Miss Johnston; Mr Bevan; Dr Mitchell, probably Alfred's own doctor; Mr R H Hulbert, occupant of Rydal Mount; Mr and Mrs W Stalker; Revd N D Thorp; Mrs Baumgartner, of Rothay Holme; Mrs Middleton; Mr Fitzgibbon, father of Una's friend, Molly Fitzgibbon; Lt Col E V Manger; Mrs MacIver of Wanlass Howe; the Misses Ashburner; George Gatey and Mr N Gatey of the solicitors, Gatey Heelis; Mr H Handley, of the same firm; Mr O Wilmot; Mr P Mason; Mr C H Wearing and Miss I Banks.

The short report of Alfred's funeral and his obituary were published as separate stories in the same edition of the *Westmorland Gazette*. Considering that Alfred was very well-known and liked locally, the report of his death lacked prominence, tucked away as it was amongst unimportant items of local news.

In the edition of the *Gazette* only the week before, one of the most important news items in terms of both prominence and column inches referred to the opening of the latest Lake Artists's Society exhibition. Five painters, including W G Collingwood, were featured; and no words of praise and admiration were too great in the paragraphs of ingratiating flattery which served as a review. Alfred's death was met with no such awe and reverence; it was as if, even at 66 years old, he hadn't quite got the artistic breeding necessary to be one of the elite, remaining, as he had always remained, just outside the boundaries of the Establishment.

"I wish you saw your way to joining the Society for that would be a practical answer to the problem..." Collingwood had written to Alfred in 1905. But Alfred stayed aloof, and his failure to join the artistic elite lost him much goodwill among fellow painters and the press, who regarded the Lake Artists as the Royal Academy of the North and its members as household names.

The obituary which appeared in the *Westmorland Gazette* concentrated on his later life in the Lake District, omitting any of his early family history at Markland Hill. However, the Bolton newspaper redressed matters by emphasising Alfred's role as one of Bolton's most famous sons, with few facts about his later life. Here are both articles, starting with the Bolton obituary:

"The death is reported from Ambleside of Mr Alfred Heaton Cooper, the well known Lakeland artist, in his 66th year. Though not a native of Bolton - he was born in Swinton - Mr Cooper can justly be claimed as belonging to the small band of artists which Bolton has produced, for he spent his boyhood here, and it was here that he began, under the encouragement of his mother, to develop his talent. His father was cashier at Messrs Cannon Bros' mill and lived in Markland Hill Lane, in one of the cottages near the path that leads across Doffcocker Lodge. As a youth, A. Heaton Cooper went to work in the Borough Treasurer's Office in the Town Hall, and members of the staff who worked with him recall that the treasurer, the late Mr Swainson, used to show young Cooper's handwriting to them as an example in neatness and clearness, of what their own should be.

He only remained in the office a few years, however, for he was already studying art assiduously and practising it as opportunity offered. In view of the intimate association of Mr Cooper's art with the Lake District, it is interesting to note that it was some watercolour drawings of Borrowdale which gained for him his first expert training in painting, three year's free tuition at the Royal Institute, London, in 1884, training which he supplemented by attendance in the evenings at life classes at the Westminter School of Art.

In 1888 he spent three months painting in Tangier and three years later he paid the first of many visits to the Norwegian Fjords. Norway provided him with a wife and a chalet in which he lived and worked at Ambleside, and which is well known to visitors to that pretty village, and that country as well as Spain, Switzerland and Ireland furnished subjects for his brush, but his best love was Lakeland. Wandering there with rucksack, sketching outfit and pipe he discovered material for most of his finest pictures. For a time after some of his foreign travels, Mr Cooper returned to Bolton and had a studio near his father's cottage at Markland Hill Lane, but in 1898 he went to the Lake District, living first at Hawkshead, then at Coniston, and settling 17 years ago at Ambleside.

Mr Cooper's pictures have always found a ready sale in Bolton, for his frequent exhibitions at Messrs Bromley's galleries have attracted all local art lovers, and many of his best subjects are to be found on the walls of homes in this district.

The Bolton obituary dwells on his beginnings rather than his life in later years, about which the writer seemed to know very little. The *Westmorland Gazette* was similarly ignorant about Alfred's origins, failing to mention Bolton or Markland Hill at all. Only by merging both obituaries does any true picture of Alfred's life and career emerge. Here is the *Westmorland Gazette* version:

Mr Alfred Heaton Cooper, the well known artist, died at his home, Cross Brow, on Sunday after a painful illness. He went to a nursing home at Lancaster but returned to Ambleside some weeks ago. He leaves a widow, two sons and two daughters and was aged 66.

He was born at Swinton, near Manchester, and he very early showed an aptitude for drawing and painting and took a delight in studying nature and the works of the great artists. He early came under the influence of Ruskin. In 1884, through submitting some watercolour drawings of Borrowdale, he gained a three year's free tuition at The Royal Institute and in the evenings attended the Westminster School of Art under Professor Brown. He adopted art as his profession at the age of 20.

Soon after finishing the course at the Westminster School, he went to Morocco and three years later he paid his first visit to Norway where the fjords subsequently provided him with so many subjects for his brush. Most of his work, however, which was influenced by the poetical naturalism of the Barbizon School, was done in the Lake District.

He first came to live in the Lake District in 1898, settling for a time at Hawkshead and then at Coniston where he erected his studio brought from Norway 22 years ago. He removed it to Ambleside in 1912 and placed it on a foundation at the end of Shady Walk. Another removal further down Lake Road has just been completed. His work has been exhibited at The Royal Academy, Liverpool since 1887 and his pictures have been hung in Paris, Petrograd, S. Africa and Australia. In 1912 he was elected a member of L'Union Internationale de Beaux Arts, Paris.

He lived and painted in Norway, Switzerland, etc but chiefly in the Lake District. A large watercolour drawing by him was purchased by Harvard University, Cambridge, Massachusets for their British art collection. He has illustrated in colour a series of books including the Lake District, Ireland, Norway, Sweden, Denmark, Norfolk & Suffolk, Northumberland, Durham, etc. He was a well-informed archaeologist and was a member of the

Westmorland Archaeological and Antiquarian Society. His wife was Miss Mathilde M. Valentinsen of Balholm, Norway whom he married in 1894.

Alfred was an elderly man when he died at the age of 66. Life expectancy was shorter in the 1920s and sixty-six years was regarded as a fair innings. Yet his work had shown no sign of ageing and never lost its vigour. He had no thoughts of retirement and his gradual development as an artist never ceased. He had so much left to paint when he died.

His coffin was laid to rest in St. Mary's Churchyard, Ambleside, in a particularly beautiful corner of that peaceful place. The big churchyard is dominated by the large Gilbert Scott church with its 180 foot spire, built in the 1850s on the highest point of the site. Grassy banks drop away from the church to the graveyard below, where Alfred's remains were buried quite close to the church, near a short, steep path linking church with churchyard. In spring the grass banks are covered with crocus and snowdrops: and in summer a tree leans out from the grass bank to shade the quiet grave. Mathilde's coffin was laid alongside Alfred's after her death in 1953.

No epitaph could be more apt than William's for his father, his teacher and painting companion:

"A rough slab of green slate marked the final resting place of my father's body, in the churchyard of St Mary's, Ambleside, but his real memorial is in the hearts of his loved ones, in his simple integrity and sunny character, and in the hundreds of vigorous landscapes he left behind all over the world". (Mountain Painter)

The epitaph on the rough slab reads, quite simply:

> *Alfred Heaton Cooper*
> *Painter of Landscape*
> *Born June 14th 1863*
> *Died July 21st 1929*
> *'God Is Love'*

Epilogue

Alfred's death was both an end and a beginning. His art was finished; but the inspiration with which he had fired his son to paint caused William to develop one of the greatest landscape talents in England this century. William's influence and inspiration has been handed down in turn to his son, Julian. Both these fine painters agree that they owe much to Alfred's hard-working attitudes to professional painting and his determination to spend his life learning how to become a better painter, however disappointing the financial reward.

After Alfred's death, Mathilde could no longer keep up the mortgage re-payments on Cross Brow, so she moved to rooms at Waterhead, facing the lake shore and boat jetties. Molly Strickland, the maid, had left because of family commitments, but after Alfred's death she returned to care for Mathilde for the next few years. Otalia moved to Chapel Stile, Little Langdale, and William was forced to return home from the south of England to run the studio and support the family, including his sister Una.

Two years after Alfred's death, Mathilde and Una decided that they wanted to move to Grasmere, which was more peaceful than Ambleside. It was the only place they would think of living, and no amount of persuasion from William could change their minds. The move meant that William had to cycle daily into Ambleside to look after the Studio, when all he really wanted to do, like his father, was to be out on the fells, painting.

In 1938 with only £120 in the bank, William, a deeply religious man, felt guided by God to sell the log cabin, for which he got £400 from an Ulverston antique dealer, in order to build a studio at Grasmere, which is still thriving today. In 1940, he married the sculptress, Ophelia Gordon Bell and the couple had four children. Two of them are currently active in the studio - Julian as a painter and John as studio manager. The Ambleside log cabin survives, its latest role being a mountaineering equipment shop.

Mathilde died at the age of 90 in 1953. Ellide and her husband, Harold Carson Parker, retired from rubber planting in South India and came to live in Torquay, where both died. Una married the poet Edmond Lee and died in Dorset in her seventies, and Frithjof also died, having never recovered fully from his war injuries. Sheila, Ellide's daughter, who used to stay at Cross Brow during her school holidays with her grandparents, died in the 1980s.

William died in 1995, at the age of 91. His son Julian continues to share his father's and grandfather's fascination for painting the natural world and its mountains, so maintaining the unique family tradition.

Alfred would surely have approved.

Grasmere Studio under construction

Grasmere Studio, 1996

150

Paintings by Alfred Heaton Cooper in Public Galleries

IN BOLTON ART GALLERY, LANCASHIRE:

Peel Hall, Little Hulton, Kenyon, oil on canvas. 1895
Exhibited at Lancashire County Council, Walkden Library, 1967

Corrie Village, Isle of Arran, oil on canvas. 1890
Exhibited at Royal Academy 1890; Liverpool, Walker Art Gallery 1890 Autumn Exhibition.

Ancient Hearth, Hawkshead, watercolour
Exhibited at the Heaton Cooper Studio, Grasmere, Exhibition of Paintings and Drawings by A. Heaton Cooper 1969.

The Black Lake - near Bergen, Norway, watercolour. 1899
presented by Mr. F. M. Hargreaves, 58 Somerset Road, Heaton, Bolton, May 1969.

Evening Sunshine, Stonethwaite, Borrowdale, watercolour. 1903
presented by Mrs. M. Harrison, The Avenue, Haulgh, Bolton, March 1968.

Wastwater Screes, watercolour and pencil
presented by Ald. C. H. Lucas, 35 Stapleton Ave., Heaton, Bolton, 1966.

Snow, Windermere from Skelgill, charcoal and pastel
Exhibited at The Heaton Cooper Studio, Grasmere, Exhibition of Paintings and Drawings by A. Heaton Cooper, 1969.

St. Sunday Crag, Ullswater, charcoal and pastel
Exhibited at the Heaton Cooper Studio, Grasmere, Exhibition of Paintings and Drawings by A. Heaton Cooper, 1969.

Raven Crag, Thirlmere watercolour
Exhibited at the Heaton Cooper Studio, Grasmere, Exhibition of Paintings and Drawings by A. Heaton Cooper, 1969.

Twilight, Whitby, watercolour
Exhibited at the Heaton Cooper Studio, Grasmere, Exhibition of Paintings and Drawings by A. Heaton Cooper, 1969.

Windermere from above Low Wood, charcoal and pastel
Exhibited at the Heaton Cooper Studio, Grasmere, Exhibition of Paintings and Drawings by A. Heaton Cooper, 1969.

Dove Crag, Hartsop, charcoal and pastel. 1922
Exhibited at the Heaton Cooper Studio, Grasmere, Exhibition of Paintings and Drawings by A. Heaton Cooper, 1969.

Rydal Water, charcoal and pastel. 1925
Exhibited at the Heaton Cooper Studio, Grasmere, Exhibition of Paintings and Drawings by A. Heaton Cooper, 1969.

Early Spring, Glenridding, watercolour
Exhibited at the Heaton Cooper Studio, Grasmere, Exhibition of Paintings and Drawings by A. Heaton Cooper, 1969.

Aberglaslyn Pass, North Wales, watercolour
Purchased from Messrs. T. Bromley & Co., Bolton, December 1926.

IN ABBOT HALL ART GALLERY, KENDAL, CUMBRIA:

Rainbow, Grasmere, watercolour
Presented by Miss Helen Reed

On the Brathay, oil on canvas
Presented by Mr James Craig

IN HEATON COOPER STUDIO, GRASMERE, CUMBRIA

Changing exhibition of paintings for sale

Paintings by Alfred Heaton Cooper
accepted for Royal Academy summer exhibitions

Year	Title
1887	Bad News from the Cape
1890	Corrie Village, Arran
1891	Glimpse of the Sea, Arran
1893	A Woodland Path - Autumn
1897	Where the Ducks Dabble - Hawkshead, Ambleside
1898	Meads and Groves of Lonsdale
1904	Coniston Fells - a February Sunset
1904	Daffodils by the Banks of the Silvery Duddon
1907	Scotch Firs and Heather, Coniston
1908	Carting Timber, Yewdale
1913	Wild Daffodils
1914	Crofters' Cottages, High Corrie, Isle of Arran
1919	Mountain Peaks of Arran
1919	Fell Foxhunting in Westmorland
1925	Ullswater - a Spring Morning

Books illustrated by Alfred Heaton Cooper

1   *The English Lakes* by W T Palmer, 1905. Reprinted 1905, 1908, 1913 (twice), 1918. 75 illustrations. A & C Black.

1a   *The English Lakes*, large version of above, limited edition 250 copies, numbered, signed A Heaton Cooper. A & C Black.

2   *The English Lakes* by Gordon Home, 1911. 12 illustrations taken from No. 1. A & C Black, "Beautiful Britain" series.

3   *The English Lake District*, 1915. Reprinted 1919, 1927, 1933. 16 illustrations, (4 new). A & C Black, "Quotation & Picture" series.

4   *English Lakes*, 1919. Reprinted 1921, 1927, 1931, 1936. 20 illustrations, taken from No. 1. A & C Black, "Watercolours" series.

5   *Wild Lakeland* by Mackenzie MacBride, 1922/1928. 32 illustrations, 9 taken from Nos. 1 & 2, 23 new. A & C Black, "Popular & New" series.

6   *The English Lakes*, 1925/1929. Reissue of W T Palmer's 1905 book. Reprinted 1936. A & C Black, "Popular & New" series.

7   *What To See in the English Lakes* by Gordon Home, 1925. 15 illustrations, taken from Nos. 1, 3 &5. A & C Black.

8   *Postcards: The English Lakes.* Series 5, 6, 6A, 7, 7A (each being a series of six cards), taken from No. 1. A & C Black.

9   *Ireland* by Frank Mathew, 1916. 50 illustrations. A & C Black, "20 Shilling" series.

10   *Ireland* by Harrison Dale, 1927. 32 illustrations, taken from No. 9. A & C Black, "Popular & New" series.

11   *Ireland* by Katharine Tynan, 1927. 8 illustrations, taken from No. 9. A & C Black, "Peeps at Many Lands" series.

12   *Isle of Man* by W Ralph Hall Caine, 1909. 20 illustrations. A & C Black, "7/6d" series.

13   *The Isle of Man* by Joseph E Morris, 1911. 12 illustrations taken from No. 12. A &C Black, "Beautiful Britain" series.

14   *Isle of Man*, 1920. 20 illustrations, taken from No. 12. A & C Black, "Watercolours" series.

15   *Isle of Wight* by A R Hope Moncrieff, 1908. 24 illustrations. A & C Black.

16   *The Isle of Wight* by G E Mitton, 1911. Repr 1920. 12 illustrations, taken from No. 15. A & C Black, "Beautiful Britain" series.

17   *Isle of Wight*, 1916. 20 illustrations, taken from No. 15. A & C Black, "Watercolours" series.

18   *Dorset* by Major H O Lock, 1925/1934. 7 illustrations (of 32). A & C Black, "Popular & New" series.

19   *Dorset*, 1936, including illustrations from No. 18. A & C Black, "Watercolours" series.

20   *Somerset* by Mrs A C Osborn Hann, 1927. 21 illustrations. A & C Black, "Popular & New" series.

21   *Somerset* 1936, including illustrations from No. 20 A & C Black, "Watercolours" series.

22   *Norfolk & Suffolk* by W G Clark, 1921. 40 illustrations. A & C Black.

23   *Norfolk* 1926. 20 illustrations, taken from No. 22. A & C Black, "Watercolours" series.

24   *Suffolk* 1926. 20 illustrations, taken from No. 22. A & C Black, "Watercolours" series.

25   *Postcards: The Broads* series 16 (6 cards) taken from No. 23. A & C Black.

26   *The Norwegian Fjords* by A Heaton Cooper, 1907. 24 illustrations. A & C Black, "Six Shilling" series.

27   *Norwegian Fjords* by A Heaton Cooper, 1914. 12 illustrations, taken from No. 26. A & C Black, "Beautiful Europe" series.

28   *Norway* by S C Hammer, 1928. 32 illustrations, some taken from No.26. A & C Black, New series.

29   *Norway* by Col A F Mockler-Ferryman, 1909. 13 illustrations, taken from No. 26. A & C Black, "Peeps at Many Lands & Cities" series.

30   *Denmark* by Clive Holland, 1928. 32 illustrations. A & C Black, "Popular & New" series.

31   *Derbyshire*, by A R Hope Moncrieff, 1927, number of illustrations unknown. A & C Black, "Popular & New" series.

32   *The County of Durham* by G E Mitton, 1924. 24 illustrations. A & C Black, "Popular & New" series.

33   *Northumberland* by Agnes Herbert, 1923. 24 illustrations. A & C Black, "Popular & New" series.

34   *Sweden* by Dudley Heathcote, 1927. 32 illustrations. A & C Black, "Popular & New" series.

35   *Reminiscences* by A Holden Illingworth, 1934(?) Privately printed.

36   *Further Reminiscences* by A Holden Illingworth, 1936. 23 illustrations. Privately printed.

Index to Text References

Abingdon, Berkshire 24, 25

Ambleside 85, 86, 98, 99, 105-108, 110, 113, 114, 116, 127, 131, 132, 136, 137, 141, 144, 146, 147, 151

    Ambleside Park 99

    Brathay Church 106

    Charlotte Mason College 99, 131

    Compston Road 109, 110

    Conservative Club 133

    Cross Brow 114-117, 131-133, 135-137, 141, 142, 144, 147

    Dove Nest 139

    Kelswick School 85

    Log cabin 73, 151

    Loughrigg 98, 102

    Millans Park 85

    Pull Woods 108

    Rothay Manor 97

    Royal Oak Hotel 133

    St Mary's Church 144, 148

    Springfield 99

    The Slack 98

    Wanlass Howe 99

    Waterhead 99, 151

Arran, Corrie 30

    Glen Sannox 30

    Loch Ranza 30

Ashburner, Misses 145

Ashworth, T 145

Aysgarth Falls 6

Bale, King 40

Ball, Professor 104

Banks, Miss I 145

Barbizon School 15, 147

Barrow-in-Furness 82

Baumgartner, Mrs 145

Bell, Ophelia Gordon 151

Benson, Oxon 25

Bevan, Mr 145

Black, A & C xii, 69, 86, 113, 126, 127, 155

Boardman, James 53

Bolton xiii, 1-5, 10, 18, 26, 29, 30, 32, 38, 40, 49, 52, 54, 58-60, 62, 82-84, 96, 141, 146, 147

    Blue Bonnet Hall 59

Daily News 84

    Doff Cocker Mill 2

    Halliwell 54

    Markland Hill 2, 3, 5, 10, 20, 28-31, 49, 54, 61, 145-147

    Over Hulton 59

Bolton-Heaton, J B 145

Borrowdale, Cumbria 10, 146, 147

Boston, USA 3

Boudin, Eugene 15

Bowfell, Cumbria 113

Bray 24, 25

Brisbane, Australia 83

Bromley, Thomas, art dealers 29, 31, 49, 96, 141, 147

Burnthwaite, Wasdale 85

Cambridge, Fitzwilliam Museum 52

    Pembroke College 52

    Ridley Hall 52

Cambridge, Massachusetts 147

Cannon Brothers, Bolton 2, 142

Carson Parker family 98, 109, 141, 144, 151

Cezanne, Paul 17

Charcoal burning 64

Clarke, WG 86

Classicism 13

Clausen, George 16-18, 128

Cleveland School of Art, Ohio 3

Cliveden Woods 25

Collingwood, W G 70-73, 146

Commissionaire, The 19

Coniston 64, 68-72, 75, 81, 85, 86, 147

    Foxhounds 87

    Institute 73

    Brantwood 70

    Crown Hotel 70

    Gate House 68

    Haws Bank

    Holywath 68

    Lanehead 72

    Mines Beck 68

    Old Man 82

    Solheim 68

    Tent Lodge 62

Yewdale Beck 63

Constable 14, 15, 18

Cookham, Berks 26

Cooper, Alice 1-3, 9, 10, 83

Cooper, Daniel 2, 10, 82, 84

Cooper, Edith 2, 10, 20, 83, 84, 135, 136

Cooper, John 2, 83

Cooper, Rachel 1, 60, 83

Cooper, Thomas, Snr 83, 84

Cooper, Thomas, Jnr 3, 4

Cooper, William, Snr 1, 2, 10, 54, 83

Cooper, William, Jnr 2, 83

Cooperhus, Balholm 75, 78

Cottam, Mrs Joan (nee MacIver) 99

Crinkle Crags, Cumbria 113

Dahl, Hans 32, 40, 48

Dallam Tower, Milnthorpe 6, 8

Deane Church 52, 54

Dedham Mill 15

Degas, Edgar 94

Delamere Forest, Cheshire 8

Denmark 117, 120, 126, 127, 147, 154

Digne, Jakob 70

Diez 15

Dorchester 25

Düsseldorf 32

Eamont, River 139

Echo de la Loire 135

Eden, River 139

Eidnes, Johannes 40

Ellis, Tristram 8

Elterwater 97

en plein air xii, 16-18, 69, 86

English Lakes, The 84, 113

English Speaking Union 117

Ese, Johannes 46

Eugen, Prince 123, 124, 127, 128

Fell, W & Co 99, 109

Fitzgibbon, Mr 145

Fitzgibbon, Molly 145

Freemasonry 52

Frithjof's Saga 40, 68,

Gatey, G 145

Gatey, N 145

Gautreau, Jean 82, 135-137

Gibraltar 26, 28

Glencoyne, Ullswater 87

Goring-on-Thames 26

Grand History of County of York 5

Grasmere xiii, 113, 117, 131, 151

Grassington 30

Graythwaite Old Hall 63

Gulf of Bothnia 125

Haines Ferry, River Thames 21, 22

Handley, H 145

Harvard University 147

Haweswater, Cumbria 8

Hawkshead, Cumbria 15, 63, 64, 147

Hawkshead, Red Lion Hotel 63

Heathcote, Dudley 117

Heaton, William 108

Heaton Cooper,

    Ellide 62, 64, 66, 69, 82, 98, 109, 131, 141, 144, 151

    Frithjof 40, 68, 82, 99, 109, 135, 137, 144, 151

    John 150

    Julian 78, 96, 151

    Mathilde 55, 57-62, 64, 66, 68, 69, 77, 81, 83, 95-97, 99-101, 103, 107, 108, 114, 116, 128, 131, 133-137, 140, 142, 144, 145, 148, 151

    Sverre 59, 60, 62

    Una 83, 99, 103, 110, 114, 131, 133 135, 137, 141, 144, 145, 151

    William xi, 2, 3, 5, 9, 57, 68, 69, 76-78, 81, 82, 88, 90, 96, 97, 99, 103, 104, 106-108, 110, 114, 131, 144, 148, 150, 151

Hebden, Yorkshire 30

Heysham, Lancs 8

Hill, David 5,6

Holland, Clive 117

Hopley, C 144

Hornby, Lancashire 6

Horwich, Lancashire 20, 52

Hulbert, R H 145

Illingworth, A H 139, 140, 144

Illingworth, Marjorie 144

Impressionism 15, 17, 18

In Turner's Footsteps 5, 6

Ince 50

Isle of Man, The 82

Isle of Wight, The 82

Jackson, J A 145

Jerome K Jerome 24

Johnston, Miss 145

Kendal Art College 107

Kilnsey Crag 30

King Haakon 77

Kvikne family 40, 48, 67, 78

Lake Artists Society 70, 72, 73, 145, 146

Lake District xi, xii, 31, 49, 62, 63, 83, 86, 96, 104, 146

Lamb, Lynton 94, 95

Leeds & Liverpool Canal 49

Lewis, Rev F 144

Linton 30

Liverpool 60, 62

Local Defence Volunteers 97

Logan, R 145

Loire, River 8, 137

London 9, 10, 13, 17, 19-22, 26, 29, 69, 103, 110, 131,
    144

    Battersea Park 19

    Cadogan Place 19

    Chelsea 19, 21

    Chelsea Bridge 21

    Cheyne Walk, Chelsea 19

    Embankment 19

    Greenwich 20

    Hyde Park 19

    Lambeth Palace 53

    Mortlake 20

    Pimlico Wharf 19

    Pool of 20

    Theatre Royal 19

Luard-Selby, Rev 144

Macbride, Mackenzie 154

MacIver family 99, 103, 145

Manchester 1, 60, 62, 140

Manger, Lt Col E V 145

Mason, P 145

Mathew, Frank 86

Maud, Queen 77

McKay, Sir George & Lady 97, 117, 135, 144

Mersey, River 29

Middleton, Mrs 145

Millet 15, 18, 22

Mitchell, Dr 145

Mitton, Ribblesdale 6

Modern Painters 6

Monet, Claude 16, 20

Montana, USA 83, 84

Moore, Henry 128

Mountain Painter xi, 148

Munich 32

Naturalism 13, 17

Newby Bridge, Cumbria 62

Newcastle 40, 49, 59, 70

Norfolk 82, 86, 114, 147

Normann, Augustin 32, 40, 48

Norske kringle 34

Norway xi, xii, 15, 31, 32, 35, 37, 38, 41, 43, 45, 48, 49,
    50, 58-60, 62, 66, 68, 69, 73, 76, 77, 84, 89, 91, 96,
    104, 108, 122, 126, 140, 146, 147

    Balestrand 31, 32, 40

    Balholm xi, 40, 41, 43-46, 48, 49, 54, 58, 60, 65, 67,
    73, 76, 77, 84, 89, 91, 96, 104, 108, 122, 126, 140
    146, 147

    Bergen 49, 140

    Bondhus Glacier, Sundal 36

    Ese Fjord 57, 77

    Folgefonn Glacier 35

    Hardanger Fjord 35, 37, 40

    Lofoten Islands 140

    Naero Fjord 47

    Odda 35

    Oppedal 38

    Rosendal 35

    Sogn 32, 40, 45-47, 68

    Sognefjord 32, 40, 47, 72

    Sor Fjord 35

    Stavanger 66

    Sundal 36

    Tjugum 44, 46, 56

    Tromso 140

    Ullensvang 35, 38, 39

    Vadheim 75

    Vik Church, Sogn 45

Norwegian Fjords, The 82, 89, 138

Norwegian Lutheran Church 44, 57

Olav, Crown Prince 77

Old Windsor 20-22, 24, 26

On Westminster Bridge 20

Oxenfell 15

Palmer, W T 70, 113

Pangbourne 26

Paris 16, 22, 83, 84, 136, 147

Preparation for Painting 94

Prisoner of Zenda, The 97

Reminiscences 139

Ribblesdale 6, 20

Rokesby 6

Rousseau 15

Royal Academy 29, 49, 50, 53, 62, 63, 96, 147

Royal Institute of Art 18, 146, 147

Ruskin, John 5, 8, 44, 70, 72, 73, 85, 147

Rydal Hall 108

Scherbatow, Prince Boris 67

Scott, Gilbert 148

Scott, J 145

Seascale, Cumberland 103

Seurat 17

Shillingford 25, 52

Sickert 94

Silverdale 8, 31

Sketching from Nature 8

Skippers Sardines 40, 108

Skipton 30

Snowdonia 140

Southport 60-63

    Lord Street 61

    Marine Lake 61

Sphere, The 71, 142

SS Fjaler 40

SS Hardangeren 34

SS Malta 26

SS Patricia 122

St Bee's School 107

St Nazaire 135-137

St Petersburg 66, 68

Stalker, Mr & Mrs W 145

Streatley 26

Strickland, Molly 131, 141, 151

Suffolk 86, 114, 147

Swan & Morgan, Newcastle 49

Sweden 117

Sweden xiii, 117, 120-122, 124-128, 146

    Gotland 124

Lappland 117, 120, 125-127

    Lulea 125

    Oland 125

    Stockholm 122-127

Swinton 1, 2, 146, 147

Tangier, Hotel Central 28

    Mosque el Kebir 28

    Mosque of the Prophet 28

    Souk 28

Tegner's *Frithjof's Saga* 40, 68

Thames, River 19-21, 24, 26, 30, 52

Thorp, Rev D N 145

Three Men in a Boat 24

Torver, Sunny Bank 63

Towlow, Frizt 16

Trondheim 70

Troutbeck 87, 99, 109

Turner, JMW 5-8, 14, 18, 26, 30

Ullswater, Glencoyne 87

Ulverston 82, 83, 85, 151

Valentinsen, Mathilde 49, 54, 148 (see Heaton Cooper)

    Otalia 83, 97, 114, 116, 131, 133, 137, 144, 151

    Rasmus 41

Wasdale, Burnthwaite 85

Watson, Angus 108

Watson, Sir William 114, 115

Wearing, C H 145

Westminster School 18, 147

Westmorland Gazette 144-147

Whaley Bridge 18

Wharfe, River 139

Whitby 139, 143

Whitchurch 23

Wibaux, Nellie 82, 84

    Pierre 83

Wigan, Lancashire 49

Wild Lakeland 113

Wilmot, O 145

Windermere, Lake 85, 99, 113

Windsor 21, 22, 24, 28

Wray Castle 108

Wraysbury 24

Young Anglers, The 6